PRAISE FOR
Running for My Life

This true story of a Sudanese child refugee who became an Olympic star is powerful proof that God gives hope to the hopeless and shines a light in the darkest places. Don't be surprised if after reading this incredible tale, you find yourself mysteriously drawn to run alongside him."

—RICHARD STEARNS, PRESIDENT, WORLD VISION US AND AUTHOR OF *THE HOLE IN OUR GOSPEL*

Lopez Lomong's story is one of true inspiration. His life is a story of courage, hard work, never giving up, and having hope where there is hopelessness all around. Lopez is a true role model.

—MICHAEL JOHNSON, OLYMPIC GOLD MEDALIST

RUNNING
FOR MY LIFE

One Lost Boy's Journey from the Killing Fields
of Sudan to the Olympic Games

LOPEZ LOMONG
WITH MARK TABB

NELSON
BOOKS

An Imprint of Thomas Nelson

Published in Nashville, Tennessee, by Nelson Books, an imprint of Thomas Nelson. Nelson Books and Thomas Nelson are registered trademarks of HarperCollins Christian Publishing, Inc.

Thomas Nelson, titles may be purchased in bulk for educational, business, fund-raising, or sales promotional use. For information, please e-mail SpecialMarkets@ ThomasNelson.com.

Scripture quotations are taken from *Holy Bible*, New Living Translation. © 1996, 2004, 2007. Used by permission of Tyndale House Publishers, Inc., Wheaton, Illinois 60189. All rights reserved.

ISBN: 978-1-59555-515-1 (hardcover)
ISBN: 978-0-7180-8144-7 (tradepaper)
ISBN: 978-1-40027-503-8 (IE)

Library of Congress Control Number: 2012937358

Printed in the United States of America

24 25 26 27 28 LBC 38 37 36 35 34

To my families in America and in South Sudan who have always believed in me. And to all the children left behind— may their voices be heard through my words.

Contents

CONTENTS

ONE

Taken!

My eyes were closed in prayer when the trucks pulled up. I heard them before I saw them. When I looked up, I saw soldiers pouring out of the back of the trucks. They appeared nervous, as though they wanted to get this over with as quickly as possible. "Everybody down! *Now!*" they shouted as they ran into the middle of the congregation. I knew our country was at war. About once a month my mother and father grabbed me and my brothers and sister and ran for shelter as bombs fell in the distance from airplanes that flew far overhead. But I had never seen a soldier until this bright, summer Sunday, and I had never expected to see soldiers invade an outdoor church service.

The soldiers continued running and shouting. Our priest tried to reason with them. "Please do not do this now," he said.

The leader of the soldiers ignored him. "We're taking the children!" he screamed.

I did not know what he meant by that. I would soon.

My parents dropped to the ground, pulling me down with them. I huddled close to my mother's side. She wrapped her arm so tightly around me that my ribs hurt. All around me people screamed and cried. I started crying too. My mother tried to calm me, but she was as frightened as I was.

Suddenly I felt a hand on my back. I looked up and saw a giant man standing over me. When you are a little boy, every adult looks like a giant. His gun was slung behind his back. A chain of bullets hung across his chest. My mother pleaded with him. "No, no, no! Don't take my boy!" The soldier did not reply. With one hand he yanked my mother's arm off me while picking me up with the other. He dragged me past the giant tree at the front of our church and toward the trucks. "Hurry up. Let's go!" he yelled. All around me, other soldiers herded boys and girls and teenagers toward the trucks, all the while yelling for everyone to speed up.

I turned around. My mother and father were off the ground, chasing after me. Tears ran down their faces. They were not alone. All across our church parents chased their children, weeping and wailing. "Please do not take our children," they begged. "Please, please, we will do anything you ask—just do not do this."

One especially giant soldier swung back around toward our crying parents. He waved his gun in the air and screamed, "One more step and we will open fire!" I could not see what happened next. I felt myself being picked up and thrown into the back of one of the trucks. I bounced off another boy and landed on the hot, dirty, metal truck bed. The truck was full of children from my church. A green canopy covered the top and sides of the truck bed, so I could not see out. Suddenly, the tailgate slammed shut and the truck lurched forward.

I did not know it at the time, but my childhood had just ended.

I was six years old.

The truck bounced down the road for three or four hours, but no one said anything to anyone else. I was too scared to start up a conversation.

I guess everyone else was too. At first we all cried, but eventually that stopped. Instead we rode along in silence, everyone wondering what was going to happen to us.

The metal truck bed burned my bare feet. I tried standing on the tops of someone else's feet to cool mine off, but he pushed me away. It was so hot inside that truck. The soldiers had tied the canopy down tight on every side to keep us from jumping out. Unfortunately, he tied it so tight that no fresh air could squeeze through. The summer sun beat down on top of the truck, making it hotter and hotter in there. The light coming through the canopy gave everyone a green tint. Road dust seeped in through holes in the bed, which made it even harder to breathe.

Sweat poured down my face and stung my eyes. My clothes were soaked. The dirt in the bed of the truck turned to mud from all the sweat pouring off so many children crammed into that small space.

This was my first trip in a truck or any kind of car. In my village, everyone walked wherever we needed to go. Everyone but me. I did not walk. I ran. My parents named me Lopepe, which in our language means "fast." As a little boy, I lived up to my name. I never did anything slow. When my mother sent me to get water, I raced down to the river with my five-liter tin can and ran back as fast as I could. When she needed salt, I ran to the neighbors' to borrow some and raced back so fast that it was almost as though she had the salt right there in our hut. Even though I ran everywhere, I always imagined traveling in a car or truck would be even better. But sitting in the stifling heat in the back of the army truck, I dreamed of running back to my village and into my mother's arms.

Bouncing along in the truck, I noticed a couple of kids lying down. I don't know if they fell asleep or just passed out. Either way, I knew I didn't want to lie down on the hot, dirty truck bed. It was not just the heat. I didn't want to spoil my Sunday best shorts and shirt my mother had put on me before we left our hut for church. I still did not fully grasp the fact that my life—the life of racing my dad to our farm and playing with my brothers and sister and going to church under the trees every Sunday—was over.

Eventually the truck's brakes squeaked loudly and we came to a stop. I did not know where we were. The back canopy flew open. Finally, a breath of fresh air. Four or five soldiers jumped in. One grabbed a boy, threw something around his head, and then dropped him down out of the truck. Before my mind could process what happened to the boy, a pair of hands grabbed me. Everything went dark as the hands wrapped a blindfold tightly around my head. It was so tight I could feel my pulse throbbing in my temples.

All at once, the hands lifted me up and tossed me through the air. Another pair of hands caught me before I hit the ground. These hands then pulled up my right hand and shoved it against a shirt in front of me. I then felt a small hand on my back, which I knew had to be the hand of another boy. "Hold on to the kid in front of you and do not drop out of line!" someone shouted.

The line started to move. I did my best to hold onto the person in front of me. From behind I heard a soldier yell, "Keep up," which was followed by a loud *thwack* and a yelp. Although I did not see it, I assume someone was smacked with the butt of a rifle for falling out of line. I tightened my grip on the shoulder in front of me and jogged to keep up. I did not want to be the next one to get hit.

Marching along I felt like one of my father's cows. When my father brought the cows in from grazing in the fields, I used to run alongside with a stick and help herd them into the pen. We had around two hundred cows, which made us very wealthy in our village. I didn't realize that we were actually quite poor. People with money in South Sudan sent their children to school in Kenya, far away from the civil war that started decades before I was born. Wealthy people did not have to worry about their children being kidnapped en masse and taken to God-knows-where. War is always far worse on the poor than the rich. Always.

I marched along blindfolded for what felt like a very long time. In truth we probably walked around fifty meters. Distances always seem longer when you cannot see where you are going. The line stopped and then moved forward much more slowly. The shirt in front of me pulled away from my hand and was gone. I reached out, feeling for it so that I could stay in line. I did not want to be beaten. Suddenly, a hand yanked the blindfold off my eyes while another hand shoved me in the back.

I stumbled forward and blinked hard. I expected the sunlight to hurt my eyes, but it didn't. Looking around, I found myself inside a thatch-roofed, one-room hut crammed full of children and teenagers. The room was dark considering it was still afternoon. There were no windows and only one door. Some light came through the thatch overhead.

I moved quickly away from the door. The soldiers there kept shoving more and more children into the one-room hut, which was already quite full. The room was smaller than my living room today, yet there had to be nearly eighty of us crammed inside. As I looked around I noticed something else: all the girls were gone. When the soldiers invaded our church, they took all the boys and girls. Now the girls were nowhere to be seen. I did not want to think about what might have happened to them.

All the boys in the hut wore the same dazed expression. No one looked familiar, even though most of those inside the room went to my church. Our church met in between several villages and served families from a wide area. Perhaps if I'd been older, I might have recognized someone, but when you are six, your life revolves primarily around your own family and those who live closest to you. At least it did for me.

Standing alone inside the crowded hut, all I could think about was my family. I wanted my mother and father to burst through the door and save me. I wanted to play with my two brothers, Abraham and John, and my sister, Grace. For some reason, on this particular Sunday, my brothers did not leave for church with me and my mom and dad. Abraham is two years older than me, while John and Grace are both younger. Abraham was going to bring John and Grace to a later service. I don't know why he decided to do that or why my parents let him. At this moment, I was glad they did. As much as I missed them and longed to see them, I was glad no one else in my family had been kidnapped by these soldiers. They might have left John and Grace because they were so young, but Abraham would be right here with me in this prison camp.

I tried to push those thoughts from my mind and concentrate on what was happening around me. The instinct to survive had already started to kick in. I did not feel hungry or thirsty even though I'd had nothing to eat or drink since I left home for church with my parents. Maybe I was in shock. I do not know. Food and water were the last things on my mind. Apparently they were the last things on the soldiers' minds as well, because they did not offer us any.

Now that my blindfold was off, I studied the soldiers at the door. When they had invaded my church, they all seemed like giants. Not anymore. Several of them appeared to be around the same age as the oldest kidnapped boys. Their uniforms were tattered and worn-out, hardly uniforms at all. Most of the soldiers were barefoot.

"They're rebel soldiers," someone behind me said. I turned, thinking he was talking to me.

"How do you know?" someone else replied.

"Look at them. You can tell by their clothes," the first boy said. I now saw this first boy was not a boy at all. He was probably one of the older ones in the room. He may have been fourteen or fifteen.

"Then why did they take us? I thought the rebels were fighting for us," the second boy replied.

"They are," the first boy said.

"That doesn't make any sense," the second boy said. "If they are the good guys, why would they kidnap all of us boys?" That's what I wanted to know too.

"Don't you see?" said the first boy. "They didn't kidnap us. We've been recruited by force to become soldiers."

That explanation seemed to make perfect sense to these two boys, but it didn't to me. I could not lift a gun, much less shoot one. How could I become a soldier? None of this made any sense to me.

"Lopepe," someone said.

I looked up.

"You're Lopepe, aren't you? From Kimotong, right?"

I was almost too afraid to answer. The boy asking the questions appeared to be around thirteen or fourteen. Two others stood next to him.

"When I saw them shove you through the door, I thought that was you," the boy said. He introduced himself and his two friends to me. They may have told me their names, but I don't remember. Every other detail of that day is burned into my mind. I can see it like it was yesterday, but I cannot remember the names of these three boys.

"We're from Kimotong too. We know your family. You have an older brother named Abraham, right?"

"Yes," I said, still wondering who these boys were and what they wanted from me.

"Is he here too?"

"No. He and my other brother and sister were coming to a later church service. I was the only one taken."

"Don't worry," said the boy. "You stick close to us and you will be all right."

"Really?" I asked. "Why would you want to look out for me?"

"We're from the same village, which makes us family."

I smiled for the first time that day. "Okay," I said. "Thank you."

For the first time since my nightmare began, I felt like I was not alone. God had sent three angels to watch over me. Soon they would do much, much more.

TWO

My Stolen Life

I hardly slept that first night in the rebel prison camp. So many boys packed the hut that I barely had room to lie down. Nor did I have a mat on which to sleep like I did at home. Instead I and all the other boys lay down on the cold, hard ground wherever we could find an open space. And it was cold by African standards. Summer days in South Sudan are hot, but the nights are very cool. I blew into my hands to try to warm them up. When that didn't work, I put them in my armpits. At home I had a small blanket to cover up with. Not here.

I could not get warm. No one could. All around me boys shivered in the cold. Instinctively, I scooted over to a boy near me and put my arms around him. He hugged me back. Before long, everyone near me was pressed against everyone else. That wasn't hard to do since we were packed into that small space like sardines. In America, boys won't get that close to another boy, no matter how tight the space. No one in that hut had a problem with snuggling against another boy and hugging him through the night. It was the only way to keep warm.

As soon as it got dark, boys began crying for their families. Everyone cried at some point in the night. The conversations started around the same time. No one dared talk loudly. Instead we whispered as softly as we could. The same conversation took place all around the room. "Why do you think they took us? What's going to happen to us now? Will they ever let us go back home? Do you think we will ever see our families again?" The whispers grew louder and louder the longer we talked. When we got too loud, a guard stuck his head inside the door and screamed, "Shut up in there!" The room fell silent for a few minutes. The only sounds were the youngest boys sobbing in the dark. Before long the whispered conversations started again. The whispers grew louder and louder until the guard screamed at us again. This went on all night.

My stomach hurt from hunger. I did not feel like eating, but my stomach told me it wanted food. I also needed to go to the restroom, but I was too afraid to ask the guards at the door where the restrooms were located. We all were that first night. My nose told me some of the boys went ahead and took care of their business anyway right there inside the hut. I didn't need to go that badly.

I closed my eyes and tried to sleep. The way I saw it, if I were asleep, I would not think about being hungry or needing to go to the restroom. When I closed my eyes, my mind floated back to my family. I saw our mud hut with its thatched roof. The fireplace on which my mom cooked during the rainy season and which we used to keep warm on cold nights was in the center of the hut. My parents slept on one side of the fire, and my brothers and sister and I slept on the other. A storage room sat off to one side, with another storage area built up high. We kept all our food up there. Sometimes when it rained, the water seeped in from outside and made the floor wet. That's why we kept the food in a high place—plus, it made it harder for little boys to sneak a snack. I loved my home. I always felt safe there. Even at night I never felt afraid. I used to drift off to sleep listening to our cows rustling around outside.

I awoke to the sound of the cows talking among themselves. They sounded angry. *How can cows talk?* I wondered as I opened my eyes. Only then did I remember how far away I was from my mat and my fireplace and my cows and my family.

The door opened on the far side of the hut. "Eat," a soldier called out. He shoved a large plastic bucket into the hut and slammed the door. All the boys rushed over to the bucket and dug in. Everyone was pushing and shoving so much that I didn't know if I would be able to get close enough to it to find out what was inside. My three teenage friends, my three angels, found me. "Follow us, Lopepe," one said. He pushed his way through the crowd. I held onto him and followed behind.

The bucket contained cooked sorghum. It is a common food in Africa. The plant looks like corn in the field, but the grain looks a lot like millet. Most people cook it into a porridge, or at least they soak the grains to soften them before they cook them. The rebel soldiers did neither. Normally cooked sorghum looks a little like oatmeal. This stuff looked like dirty mush.

When the soldiers slopped the sorghum into the bucket, they didn't even drain off the excess water. It looked disgusting, but I was too hungry to care. I plunged both hands into the bucket and grabbed all my hands could hold. I sat down not far from the bucket and shoveled the grains into my mouth as fast as I could. Something hard crunched between my teeth. I spit it out, then went right back to shoveling food in. "Slow down, Lopepe," my friend said. "This stuff is half sand. Eat it like this." He sifted through the sorghum and ate grains individually. Other boys around the room weren't as careful. A short time after we finished eating, I noticed several holding their stomachs and groaning. The food had made them sick.

A boy went over and knocked on the door. The guard opened it slightly. "I need to go to the restroom," the boy said. He was a little older than me, but not much.

"Oh you do, do you?" the guard said.

"Yes sir, very badly," the boy said.

The guard reached in and yanked the boy out by the arm. I heard the sound of a cane crashing down on the boy. I'd heard the sound before, but never on a boy. Farmers used canes to keep their cattle in line. The boy cried out, but the cane kept slapping down on him until he had received ten whacks. A short time later the sound echoed through the hut a second time. The door flew open, and the boy tumbled back inside. Blood ran down from a split lip, and his eye had nearly swollen shut.

"What did they do to you?" someone called out.

"They beat me as soon as they dragged me outside," he said. "They said I was trying to escape and they wanted to show me what they did to anyone who tried to escape. Then they led me out into the woods at gunpoint. I did my business and never acted like I was going to run away. That didn't matter. They led me back at gunpoint and beat me again before throwing me back in here."

Everyone must not have heard his story because other boys went to the guard to go to the restroom. They all came back bleeding and bruised. It didn't take long for us to figure out that we shouldn't ask to go out to the restroom. Instead, everyone just went inside the hut wherever they could. Before long the smell was overwhelming, but what could we do? None of us wanted to be beaten up by soldiers every time we had to go to the restroom.

Days went by. The first day became routine. Soldiers never came inside the hut. Each morning they shoved food through the door for us. The food never changed: cooked sorghum mixed with sand. Desperate boys devoured both. We placed the empty bucket beside the door when we were finished, and someone reached in and took it away. The rest of the day we sat and did nothing until night fell. Then we slept in the cold, huddled up against one another, waiting for the sun to come up and warm us.

By the third or fourth day I noticed something new: not everyone got up when it was time to eat our one meal. At first I thought these boys were sleeping in, which surprised me because it was so hard to sleep in these conditions. Looking closer I noticed these sleepy boys did not stir at all. They were dead. I'd never seen a dead boy before. I wanted to cry, but I did not dare. Instead I sat and stared at the dead boys, horrified, wondering if that would be me soon.

Soldiers entered the room a short time later, one of the rare occasions when they actually came inside the prison hut. They carried the dead boys outside and slammed the door. That's the last I saw of those dead boys, but they were not the last to die. Every morning boys did not wake up. More than once I went off in search of a friend I'd made the day before, only to discover he was one of the ones who did not wake up.

After a few days of boys dying, I heard shouting outside. The room became quiet. We all wanted to hear what was going on.

"Why are we keeping these boys if they're dying on us like this?" a man yelled.

"We thought we needed more time to break their wills before we start the training," someone replied.

"If you wait much longer, they'll all be dead. Get it started. *Now!*"

"But some of them are too small."

"How is that my problem?" the man shouted back. "Pull out the ones strong enough to hold a rifle and start training them."

"What about the rest?"

"What about them?" the man snapped back. "The way things are going in there, we won't have to worry about them much longer anyway."

The conversation ended. The door flew open. Five or six soldiers came in, angry. Each one grabbed a boy and sized him up. They pushed the older boys toward the door, where another soldier took charge of them. The rest were shoved toward the far side of the room.

A soldier came up to me. He didn't even bother looking me over. Immediately he grabbed my shoulders, turned me toward the rejection pile, and shoved me out of his way. "Over there!" he yelled and then moved on to the next boy.

My three angels were standing near me when the soldiers stormed in. The soldiers pushed all three of them toward the door. One of them made eye contact with me before he left the hut. He nodded. I guess he wanted to let me know that everything would be all right. I didn't know if I would see him again. None of us knew what was happening.

I walked over to the rejects, most of whom were still older than me. We sat and waited. When the soldiers finished with the last boy, they stormed out of the hut and slammed the door behind them. Many of the boys left behind began to cry. I moved over by the wall to try to hear what was going on outside. All I could hear was yelling and the sound of people running around here and there. Later I heard gunfire, which was followed by more yelling and running.

Eventually the crying stopped. I struck up a conversation with one of the other boys. That's how I am. I love to talk and to talk a lot. Not everyone was so talkative, but before long we not only talked, but we made up games. It beat sitting and crying. We were still boys, after all.

That evening, the door opened, and the boys who were taken out earlier in the day returned. I watched for my three angels. The moment they walked through the door, I ran over to them.

"Don't worry," one of them said to me. "We won't go anywhere without you." That made me feel better, although, given what was going on around us, I did not know how they could deliver on their promise.

That night the room was alive with new conversations. Boys talked about the training. I could tell some of them were into it. Their voices got excited when they talked about shooting an AK-47. Although I had no desire to shoot a gun, I envied them because they at least got to go outside. I had not left the hut in all my days in the rebel prison camp.

The next morning after our one meal, the soldiers came back into the hut and separated the strong boys from the young and weak. Like the day before, I was in the latter group. The strong ones spent their day training to become soldiers. The rest of us tried to keep ourselves busy. Every morning I did my best to clean up my small corner of the hut. I swept it and carried off any garbage that happened to fall in my spot. It wasn't much, but I had to find something to do to fill my time.

Back at home, I bugged my parents constantly to let me help. When I asked my dad to let me go to the farm with him, he said, "No, you're too small. Stay home with your mother." I did not take no for an answer. I ran as fast as I could to the farm. When my dad walked up, I was already there. He was right. I was too small to do most of the work, but I did what I could. Working made me very happy, especially working alongside my father on the farm.

Keep in mind, farming in South Sudan is not like farming in the United States. There, everything is done by hand, from breaking up and plowing the ground with long poles, to planting the seed, to harvesting the grain. When I came to the United States and saw tractors and combines for the first time, I wondered why we did not have those in Sudan. If we did, no one would ever go hungry.

On the days I did not go to the farm, I followed my mother around and did whatever I could to help her. If she was in the kitchen cooking, I was in the kitchen asking, "What can I do to help?"

"Lopepe," she said to me, "boys are not supposed to be in the kitchen. Go outside with your friends."

"No, Mother, I want to help you," I said.

My mom looked down at me, smiled, and said, "Okay, stir this," or, "Run over to the neighbor and borrow some salt." When she didn't have anything else for me to do, I went out in the forest and scavenged for vegetables. I was very close to my mother and father. Every day I loved the love they poured out on me. I was a very happy boy.

I didn't work every day. My friends and I spent many a day playing hide-and-seek in the forest until the sun went down without a care in the world. Whenever we bored of hide-and-seek, we made up other games. Sometimes we let the girls in on the fun and played house with them. We boys became men. "I'm going hunting," we'd tell the girls and go back to the forest. When we returned, we dropped our "kill" in front of them. The kill usually consisted of a big rock. The girls pretended to clean and cook the rock, while we boys sat down in the hut, propped up our feet, and rested from our hard day in the forest, just like we saw our dads do in the evening. It was a good life. As a small boy in a small village in a remote section of Sudan, I thought everyone in the world lived this way.

Now I found myself in a very dark place with nothing to do. If I spent too much time thinking about home and my mom and dad, all I wanted to do was cry. I figured out very quickly that I could not do that and survive.

As the days went by, the number of boys in my group grew smaller and smaller. The soldiers did not take any of us out for training and our group grew smaller because boys kept dying. I did not sit and stare in horror at the dead boys any longer. Death was just a part of life in the prison camp. With time, I got used to it.

I got used to most things in the prison camp. Before long, I had no trouble going to sleep at night. Some mornings I slept right through the strong boys leaving to go out and train. I got used to picking through my sorghum every day, separating the grains from the sand. I got used to being left in the weak group where the soldiers waited for us to die. I got used to not feeling the sunshine on my skin or breathing fresh air.

But I never got used to the smell. With each passing day the place stunk worse and worse.

Some changes began to take place around me though. The strong boys, who started out as captives like me, became more and more like

16

the soldiers who brought us here. The way they walked, the way they talked, and the way they looked at the young and weak became indistinguishable from the soldiers outside the hut. I could tell many of these boys liked the idea of becoming rebel soldiers. The guards did not have to separate us each morning. These boys were up waiting to go out and train and shoot.

My three angels were not like that. They went outside for the training just like all the rest, but it was just an act.

For others, though, it was not an act. The transformation for these boys was nearly complete. Soon they would be soldiers, ready to go off and fight. The question now was, when their training was complete, what would become of the boys left behind?

What would they do with me?

THREE

Escaping with the Angels

Y ou're going to see your mom again."

"What?" I nearly shouted.

"Shh, not so loud," one of my three teenage friends said. "You can't tell anyone." He looked around the room. Most of the boys had settled down for the night, although one or two were up walking around. "This is our secret, okay, Lopepe?"

"I won't say a word."

My friend gave me a look.

"No, really. I know I talk a lot, but I won't say anything. I promise."

"Good. You won't have to keep the secret for long," he said with a grin. "Come here." He motioned for me to come between the three of them. "Sleep over here between us tonight."

"Okay," I said. Since we slept on the floor, one spot was about the same as any other. By now, I was used to sleeping on the cold floor.

However, on this night, I was so excited I could hardly go to sleep. *I'm going to see my mom again!* It felt as though I had not seen her in years, when in reality only three weeks had passed since the soldiers invaded our

19

church service. *It won't be much longer!* I told myself over and over. The more I thought about home, the more excited I became and the harder it was for me to sleep.

Because I was six years old, I did not think to ask the obvious. Even at six, I should have asked how I was going to get to see her again. *How* did not matter. My friends, my three angels, told me I was going to see her, and that was good enough for me.

My eyes finally grew heavy and I slipped off to sleep. I awoke to someone shaking me. I opened my eyes and started to speak, but my angels held fingers over their mouths. "Shh, don't say a word," one whispered so softly I could hardly hear him. He motioned for me to stand. I did what I was told. No one else in the hut stirred. The air was full of the sounds of deep breathing as all the boys slept very soundly.

Even though several boys had died during the past three weeks, we were still packed tightly in the hut. Once everyone lay down, there was barely room to move. That did not stop my three angels. The first stepped over a sleeping boy, gently placing his foot on the far side, and then he pulled himself over. He reached out his arms. The second boy picked me up and handed me across. The first boy set me down in the small sliver of space between the sleeping boys. The next one stepped over to us and then climbed over the next sleeping boy. They passed me across and repeated the process again and again toward the door.

Over the next ten or fifteen minutes, we worked our way across the room. Once we reached the door, we stopped dead still. My three friends leaned with their ears toward the door and outside wall. After what felt like an eternity, one nodded toward another. He reached over and opened the door ever so slightly. Normally, any time the door moved so much as an inch, it whined with a loud creak. Not on this night. Real angels were with us. God kept the door from creaking.

One of my friends poked his head out the door for a quick look around. The coast was clear. The guard who normally sat at the door had left his post. My friend opened the door just wide enough for us to squeeze through. One went outside, then another. I started to jump through the doorway after him. I wanted to get out fast before the guard returned, but my friend at the door motioned for me to get down flat on the ground. I did as I was told. I pressed myself against the ground as low as I possibly could and slithered through the doorway into the night air.

Nothing ever smelled as sweet as the air outside that doorway. Over the past three weeks, the prison hut had turned into a foul-smelling toilet. For the first time since I was blindfolded out of the back of the truck, fresh air filled my nose. I had almost forgotten what it smelled like.

I didn't have time to take in the moment. My two friends who were already outside pulled me between them. The third quickly joined us. The door behind us was closed. Again, it did not make a sound. Its familiar squeak fell silent.

One of my friends pointed along the side of the hut and swept his hand in an arc. The others nodded like they understood. I did not. I didn't need to. One pushed me flat against the ground, then mouthed, "Follow me." Off we went, crawling flat on our bellies along the side of the hut like cobras through the grass. All around us voices talked and laughed and cursed. My friends did not seem to notice. They kept crawling.

I looked up and saw little orange circles in the night perhaps ten or fifteen feet away from me. Then I heard the sound of a match striking hard against something. My eyes went immediately toward the flame. I watched as it went up, then it lit up a face of one of the guards. He held the flame up to a cigarette, lit it, and then let the match fall to the ground.

A hand pressed down on my head. I glanced to the side. One of my friends shook his head at me. He mouthed, "Stay down."

I nodded and kept on crawling after him.

A soldier laughed. He sounded like he was standing right on top of me. I wanted to look up but I froze instead. My friends on either side of me pulled me along. I kept going. The guards' voices seemed to get louder and louder. I could not see them—only the nearby glow of their

21

cigarettes. And they could not see us in the moonless night. We blended into the darkness.

The guards kept talking and laughing, and I kept crawling. No one said it, but we all knew the guards would open fire on us if they found us trying to escape. We did not care. I would rather die trying to escape than to sit and wait for death to come find me inside that prison hut.

We crawled past the hut. I glanced up and noticed the faint outline of a fence just beyond us. It was hard to see in the dark. I do not know how my friends knew where to go. We crawled closer to the fence. Perhaps ten minutes had passed since we slipped out the hut door. My heart beat in my ears.

Once we were right upon the fence, I saw a very small gap in the bottom of it. One of my friends climbed through the hole. I could not believe the guards couldn't hear the clanking of the chain-link fence. However, like the squeaking door that fell silent on this night, I know God Himself was responsible for the guards not hearing us. I thought of the story in the book of Acts where angels set Peter free from prison in the middle of the night. The angel made the chains drop from Peter's wrists and then threw open the prison gate. Peter walked right out of the prison and not one of the guards noticed. God did the same thing for me and my three angels that night.

My friend held the fence open and motioned for me. I slipped right through. From the other side I looked back toward the hut. The glowing orange circles all seemed to be on the opposite side of the compound from us. My next friend struggled through the hole. It was so small, I don't know how any of them made it through it. I remembered a story my mother had told me from the Bible. She told me that Jesus said it was easier for a camel to go through the eye of a needle than for a rich man to get into heaven. "That's why it is so important for us to sacrifice cows to give thanks to God," she said. "Our cows are what make us rich." Her words rang in my ears that night. The hole in that fence was the eye of the needle I had to pass through to be saved.

My third friend forced himself through the hole. The moment he was through, two friends grabbed me on either side, and we ran for our lives. I moved my legs as fast as I could, trying to keep up. When I couldn't keep up, my friends lifted me off the ground and carried me along. None of us wore shoes. Rocks cut into the soles of my feet. We kept running. Bushes suddenly appeared in front of us. We hardly slowed down. The branches reached out and slapped at my legs. Thorns tore my skin open. I barely felt a thing. We kept running. And running. And running.

I listened for the sound of soldiers chasing after us, but all I could hear was my heart banging in my chest and my heavy breathing. My legs started to give out. Even with a friend helping me on each side, I could not keep going. One boy paused for a moment. Reaching around me, he swept me on his back and off we went. Big trees came up over us. I knew a lion or a leopard might be hiding in one, waiting for an antelope to come by. My friends didn't even look up. They kept on running, carrying me with them.

The forest disappeared behind us. My friend lowered me down so that I could run on my own. Tall savannah grass enveloped us. We found a game trail and ran and ran and ran. My legs gave out and I stumbled and fell. My friends helped me to my feet. "Just a little while longer, Lopepe, and we will stop to rest," he said.

"Okay," I muttered. I could hardly speak.

We ran through the tall grass. Hours had passed since we slipped through the eye of the needle, and still we ran. I do not know how we could run so far and so fast and so long. We did not run with our own strength but with strength from God. That is the only explanation.

The sky above our heads turned from pitch-black to midnight blue. Soon the sun would be up. My friends slowed down. One took off a little ways off the path. A few moments later he came back and motioned for the rest of us. Another picked me up and carried me through the tall grass. The third boy walked behind him, fluffing up the grass behind us to hide our trail from anyone chasing us.

The four of us collapsed on a bed of grass about fifteen or twenty yards from the trail. "Rest," one said.

I fell back onto the soft grass. It felt so much better than the hard hut floor. The sky grew lighter. I looked down at my legs. Dried blood covered them. One month earlier I would have cried over such a sight. Not now. Bleeding legs was a small price to pay to be free. "That way," one of my angels said as he pointed into the distance. "Everyone lie down facing that direction."

"Why?" I yawned.

"That's the direction we will run after we rest. It is easy to get turned around out here. If we are not careful, we may end up running right back to the prison camp."

"I don't ever want to see that place again," I said.

My angel smiled. "Don't worry," he said. "You won't."

I did not reply. My eyes grew very, very heavy. I fell asleep and dreamed of home.

FOUR

Running Home

I woke up running. Something must have happened on my first morning of freedom before we took off running under the bright, hot, summer African sun, but I do not remember it. I opened my eyes and found myself between two of my friends, running as fast as I could go down a game trail with tall grass and an occasional acacia tree flying past us.

My feet screamed in pain with every step, but I did not dare listen to them. Somewhere up ahead my mother waited for me. I would not slow down until I found her. My tongue stuck to the roof of my mouth. I hadn't had anything to drink in over a day, but I didn't complain. I had gone even longer without water when the rebel soldiers kidnapped me. If this was the price I had to pay to be free, so be it. I could do this.

The sun pushed down on top of me, trying to shove me down to the ground. We stayed as close to the occasional tree as we could. Every small bit of shade gave me an extra spring in my step. But running under the midday sun was much harder than running the night before. I did not know how I kept going. I tried to focus on the scenery around me to take my mind off being thirsty. A herd of gazelles bounced along in the distance as if they did not have a care in the world. I wished I could run like them—then I would be home in no time.

Our game trail took us near a hill. We ran along the side of it for a short distance before coming upon a cave. My three friends stopped at the mouth of the cave. I stopped as well. All of us struggled to catch our breath. When I saw how worn-out my angels were, I felt a little better. I was afraid I was slowing us down.

"We won't last long in this sun," one said. "We ought to rest in here until the sun starts to go down."

The others nodded in agreement. Like me, they were too winded to speak. Eventually one of them spit out, "We need to find some water."

"Agreed," the other said. "You think those gazelles we saw could have been on their way to a water hole?"

"It's worth checking out," the third said. "I'll go see what I can find."

I collapsed on the ground in the cave. My feet throbbed. Dirt caked with blood filled the cuts on my soles. Still, I did not complain or say anything about hurting. These throbbing feet were taking me home.

I lay back and closed my eyes. My body ached, but my mind ran straight to home. I saw my mother standing next to the fire while my father came in from the fields, herding his cattle. My brothers played nearby. They smiled when they saw me. "Welcome home, Lopepe," they said. "We've been waiting for you."

A hand shook me awake. "Here you go," a voice said. I opened my eyes. The boy who had gone off in search of water held what appeared to be a rolled-up banana leaf in front of me. "Drink," he said. He held the leaf to my mouth and tipped it back. I've never tasted anything as cool and wonderful as that drink of water. One of the other two boys then took off. When he returned, the third left. Both brought me back more water.

We stayed in the cave the rest of the day. I slept off and on the entire time. When the shadows outside grew long, we took off. We'd only gone a short way when my stomach started growling. It had been a long time since our last meal of soggy sorghum mixed with sand. My stomach growled so loudly that the boys on either side of me laughed. About that time we passed trees with low-hanging fruit that looked sort of like plums. We stopped long enough to eat our fill. Then we took off again.

The fact that we found both food and water just when we needed it did not strike me as remarkable at the time. Nor did I find it amazing the next day and the day after that when it happened again. My mother had taught me the story of the children of Israel wandering through the wilderness for forty years. "God gave them manna in the morning, and when Moses hit a rock with his stick, water came out," she told me. What God did for the Israelites in the Bible He did for me and my friends in our wilderness trek. I may have been far from home, but He had not abandoned me. I never doubted that for a moment.

The sky grew dark. Stars came out. We ran and then we ran some more. The moon rose. We came upon a road that we had to cross. Three of us hid in the grass while one of my angels crept close to the road to look for coming cars. Once he was certain we would not be seen, we dashed across as quickly as possible. The last boy used a tree branch to wipe away our footprints. He did the same thing every time we crossed roads over the next couple of days. We crossed several, but we never saw any car or truck. For that matter, we never saw any signs of another human being. It was as though we were the only four people in this little corner of South Sudan.

We ran through the night, stopping only long enough to catch our breath or grab a drink of water when we happened upon an oasis. The next morning we ran until the sun got too hot to continue. Only then did we find a shady place to hide and rest. Once again, we lay down facing the direction we needed to go when we started running again.

I felt miserable. The pains in my feet and legs had spread to my entire body. Even so, I didn't have any trouble going to sleep. The moment my body hit the ground, I passed out. I didn't stir until one of the angels nudged me and said, "It's time to get going."

The sun comes up at six every morning in equatorial east Africa and goes down exactly twelve hours later. We didn't wait for it to go down before taking off. Just like the day before, we started running when the shadows grew long and the sun was low in the sky.

The next night of running was a carbon copy of the one before and the one before that. The terrain never changed. From late afternoon into night and on into the next morning, we ran through an endless sea of savannah grass punctuated by islands of acacia trees. We stayed in the bush the best we could, although there were times we had to sprint out in the open to cross a road. When we did, we stayed as low to the ground as possible and ran as fast as our legs would carry us.

By the time the sky turned light, our legs did not want to move. All four of us were starting to break down. I wanted to stop. I needed to stop. I cannot describe the pain shooting up from the soles of my feet with every step I took. Running through broken glass could not have hurt more. My friends struggled to keep going as well. But we could not stop. Not yet. I knew if I sat down, I would not get back up.

I'm not sure you can call what we did at this point running, but we tried. Head down, one step in front of another as fast as I could move, I pressed on. Home had to be just ahead. I felt like I was running in a fog. Unlike the first night, the other boys did not have the strength to put me on one of their backs and carry me. I had to carry myself on my own two feet.

The tall grass gave way to open fields. We had no choice but to cross. We could not turn back.

Suddenly, we came upon a tin-roofed building. A couple of trucks were parked next to it, along with a car. I heard voices, men's voices, but I could not understand what they said. They did not speak Buya, the language of my tribe, or any language I'd heard in my life. My mind was still trying to make sense of the words flying through the air when

I saw them: soldiers. However, these soldiers wore real uniforms, not the worn-out rags of the rebels. They could not be the ones hunting us. However, we could not take that chance. "Down on the ground," one of my friends said.

But it was too late. The soldiers saw us. They bolted in our direction. My friends and I looked around desperately, but there was no place for us to hide. The soldiers came closer. I wanted to run, but my legs gave out. I fell to the ground, and I could not get back up. The soldiers rushed upon us. I looked at my friends. They could not move either. We were caught. After three nights of running through the wilderness, we were caught.

Three or four soldiers came up and started firing off questions, one after another. We could not understand a word they said. One of my friends said to them, "We were taken by rebels. Please, we just want to go home." They did not understand him any better than we understood them. The questions kept coming. The four of us had to look silly, sitting there, unable to communicate. The questions stopped. The soldiers talked among themselves. They pointed at us, made motions in the distance, and then talked some more.

However, they did not use a threatening tone with us. We had been arrested, but these were not Sudanese rebels or Sudanese army soldiers. The whole time we thought we were running toward our village, we were in fact running straight to Kenya. These soldiers were Kenyan border guards. And they knew who we were. They'd come to recognize the rail-thin build and the rags on our backs as distinguishing marks of boys escaping the civil war in Sudan.

Another soldier came up with a bucket. He dipped out a ladle of water for me. I tried to stand up, but I could not. No matter how hard I tried, my legs refused to work. He lowered the ladle down to me and let me drink my fill. The other boys drank their fill of water as well. Another man handed us a small dish with some corn in it. I looked at it very closely. There wasn't any sand mixed in. I scooped part of it up and shoved it into my pocket. The rest I gulped down.

"It's not home, Lopepe," one of my friends said, "but at least we are safe. Don't worry. We will get you to your mother somehow."

"I know," I said. "I know."

I looked closely at the faces of my three angels. Each of them looked like a runner who falls across the finish line, completely exhausted, with nothing left to give. That's what the Kenyan border felt like. It felt like stumbling across the finish line of the longest, most grueling race in the world. I can only imagine how I looked to them. My clothes, my Sunday best shirt and shorts just a few weeks earlier, were now shredded. What little material remained was caked with dirt and blood.

A soldier motioned for us to follow him. My friends managed to walk toward a truck. I scooted along on my rear after them. It was the best I could do. The truck looked similar to those the rebels threw us into when they invaded our church. However, its paint looked much newer. The bed was clean, as was the canopy overhead. The soldiers lifted us into the back. When we sat down, no one closed the canopy tight around the back.

The truck took off down the road. Now that we were in Kenya, the road was smooth and paved. Air flowed through the truck, which was a welcome relief from the heat. "Where do you think they are taking us?" I asked.

"I don't know," one of my three friends replied, "but it is not back to the rebel camp."

"How do you know?" I asked.

"The road," he said. "It's too smooth."

I drifted in and out of sleep as the truck swayed along down the road. I awoke completely when it slowed then stopped. Outside the truck I saw a sign with letters I did not recognize. I did not know it, but the sign said "UNHCR"—that is, United Nations High Commissioner for Refugees. The driver of the truck walked over toward a very different-looking building. It was not made of mud like the huts in my village. A man came out of the building. My eyes grew wide at the sight of him.

I'd never actually seen a person like this, although he looked a lot like a picture I once saw in church.

This man with the white skin must be next to God, I thought, *because he looks like Jesus!* This was how I was introduced to Kakuma, the refugee camp that was to be my world for the next ten years.

FIVE

Kakuma

Life in my village of Kimotong is nearly the same today as it was hundreds of years ago. Most of the houses have mud walls and a grass roof. Women in our village fetch water from a nearby river. Indoor plumbing remains the stuff of science fiction in Kimotong, as do electricity and computers and television. Everyone in our village feeds their families through farming, but the farms are nothing like they are in the United States and Europe. As I mentioned, my father uses a long pole to break up the soil on our farm, as does every other farmer across this part of Africa. We shove the seeds in the ground by hand, and we harvest our grain the same way. We don't have a plow to hitch to an ox, much less a tractor or a combine to drive.

My only glimpse of the modern world came when I caught sight of a passenger airplane flying high in the sky. I did not know these planes carried people. All I knew was that they flew much higher than those that dropped bombs on nearby villages. A glimpse of one up in the top of the sky, silently spitting out a trail of clouds, left me staring wide-eyed, my mouth hanging open. "How can something fly so high?" I asked my dad.

"I do not know, Lopepe," he said. "But one day your mother and I will send you to school, where you will learn the answers to all your questions."

We did not have a school in our village. Neither my mother nor father could read or write. Very few people in our village could. A few lucky families in other villages scraped together enough money to send their children to a boarding school in Kenya, but the rest of us were out of luck in terms of getting an education. I knew my parents dreamed of sending me and my brothers and sister to school, but it was an impossible dream. No one in our village could afford such a luxury.

When the Kenyan border guards dropped off me and my three friends at the UN refugee camp, I wondered if this might have been the school my father talked about. Kakuma offered classes that any boy in the camp could attend. I learned about the school not long after I arrived. I learned lots of things those first few weeks. First and foremost, I learned what it meant to be a refugee. From the moment I stepped into Kakuma, I became a boy without a country. A refugee camp is a kind of no-man's-land. No one lives there by choice. You end up in places like Kakuma when you have no better option. Everyone who lived there just wanted to go home.

Kakuma was a tent city filled primarily with boys like me, boys from Sudan who'd been separated from their families by civil war. Some had been turned into soldiers. Others came here because their villages had been destroyed in the fighting. None of us belonged here. Yet here we were, far from home, in a country to which we did not belong. I am grateful that Kenya gave boys like me a place to escape war. The border guards who arrested me and my three angels could well have forced us to walk back to where we came from. Even worse, they could have handed us over to the rebels. Instead, they let us stay in their country.

However, it doesn't take long for refugees to figure out that they are not the only ones who wish they could go home. I sensed resentment from people who lived near the camp, especially after a famine hit Kenya. Kenyan law prohibited us from moving out of the camp and permanently settling in the country. It also made it illegal for us to take a job outside the camp. Kakuma was created as a temporary place where displaced people would be safe until the war in Sudan ended. Today, twenty years later, fifty thousand people not only from Sudan but also from Somalia, Ethiopia, Burundi, the Democratic Republic of Congo, Eritrea, Uganda, and Rwanda call Kakuma home.

It took three weeks for my feet to heal after the truck brought my friends and me to the refugee camp. About the time I could walk, my friends, my three angels, disappeared. To this day I do not know what happened to them. I got up one morning and they were gone. I thought they must have tried to walk back to our village, since that's where we thought we were going when we escaped the prison camp. Since I had such a difficult time with the first trip, I understand why they did not take me with them. Knowing these boys as well as I did, I think they planned to tell my family where I was so that my mother and father could come and get me.

But that never happened.

The three teenage boys who saved my life were never heard from again. I've tried to find them on the trips I have taken back to Sudan over the past few years. No one in my village or the surrounding area has any idea who they were. It is as if they simply appeared in the prison camp, took care of me, led me to freedom, and then disappeared, just like angels in the Bible.

With my friends gone, I had to find other boys to live with. I packed up my stuff and went to another tent of boys. "Can I live with you guys? I am all by myself," I said.

"How long have you been here?" they asked.

"Three weeks."

"Do you have a ration card?"

"Yes."

"You'll have to do chores around here, just like the rest of us."

"That's fine with me. I am not afraid to work."

With that, I had a new home. I lived in a tent of ten boys in camp section fifty-eight. Kakuma was portioned into sections for different tribes and nationalities. I lived in the equatorian section of the camp. That's the region of Sudan where I and the other boys in this section all came from.

It didn't take long for the boys in my tent to become my new family. All of us looked out for one another and shared what little we had with one another. Once a month the UN called our names for the food distribution. I lined up with all the rest of the boys, held out a ration card, and received a bag filled with grain, some oil, and a little sugar and salt. When I got back to my tent, I combined my rations with those of the rest of the boys. It was the only way we could keep what we had from being stolen.

Right after the food distribution was the most dangerous time for a young boy in the camp. Older boys, boys who were now men of eighteen or twenty years old, from other tribes in other parts of the camp would go from tent to tent, stealing food from the younger, weaker boys. My family of boys in the refugee camp did not have to worry about that. We dug a hole in the middle of our tent, hid our food down inside, then covered our stash with a mud lid someone had made. After that, we covered the whole thing with dirt. A thief busted into our tent and yelled, "Give me your food!" We all looked up at him with pathetic faces. "Someone already stole it all," we cried. The bully turned the tent upside down, looking for our stash, but he never found it. Not one of us ever breathed a word about where our food was hidden. We were too smart for that.

I am not proud to say that I envied these big boys, the ones strong enough to take whatever they wanted. They didn't eat the food they stole from others. They sold it to people outside the camp. That gave these boys something few of us had: real money. The more I watched the strong take whatever they wanted without suffering consequences from their actions, the more I looked forward to the day I would be big enough to do the same. This became my goal in life. In the refugee camp, there was no higher aspiration.

Even with pooling our rations, we only had enough grain for one meal a day. Six days a week we ate our meal in the middle of the night. That way, we were the hungriest when we needed our strength the least.

Yes, six days a week we ate only one meal, but one day was different. Every Tuesday around noon, workers left the fenced UN compound and pushed wheelbarrows to the far side of the camp. Every boy in the place listened for the *squeak, squeak, squeak* of the wheelbarrows rolling through the camp. When we heard it, we all took off running.

I had no idea what was happening the first time I heard the *squeak, squeak, squeak* go by. The boys in my tent rushed out and yelled back at me, "Hurry up, Lopepe! You don't want to miss out on this!" I raced to catch up with them. We ran across the camp until we came to a pit. Inside the pit was the garbage dump.

The moment a UN worker emptied the first wheelbarrow over the edge into the dump, mayhem broke out. Boys jumped down into the pit and dug through the garbage as quickly as they could. Elbows flew; fights broke out. Boys went after the garbage like hungry hyenas fighting over a gazelle carcass. One of the boys from my tent popped up from the pit, handed me a half-eaten banana, and said, "Get it back to the tent and don't let anything happen to it." I did what I was told. That was part of life in my camp family. We all had chores to do, roles to play, and we all did them. I guarded that banana like it was the crown jewels of England.

It didn't take very many Tuesdays for me to go from running salvaged food back to the tent, to jumping down into the scrum myself. Even though I was small, I could take care of myself. When an elbow flew in my direction, I ducked out of the way and delivered an elbow right back. My family worked together as a team down in that pit. We fought against the other boys for ripe mangoes and half-eaten pieces of bread, bananas, scraps of meat, you name it. If the Americans working in the UN compound ate it (and all the white people working there were Americans in our eyes, no matter what country they came from), they always threw part of it away. When they did, we found it. Yes, Tuesdays were the high point of our week, the one day we ate well—the day we ate garbage.

Eating garbage was not the only adjustment I made growing up in Kakuma. When I arrived, I only spoke Buya, the language of my tribe in Sudan. Everyone in the camp spoke Swahili. Within a matter of months, I spoke Swahili as well as any of them. With time I forgot how to speak Buya completely.

I also had to adjust to the fact that death was a regular part of life. In Kakuma, boys got sick and died every day. Whenever boys died, we always said malaria got them. They may have died of starvation, since food was hard to come by, especially after famine struck Kenya and the UN cut our food ration in half, but we didn't talk about that. We also didn't want to think that they may have died from the unsanitary conditions in the camp. We did not have a latrine for the ever-growing number of boys in the camp. Instead we used a dry creek bed that ran through the middle of Kakuma as our toilet. During the rainy season, the creek filled up with water and became our swimming hole. We should have known better, and maybe we did, but we swam there all the same. Swimming in the latrine caused disease to spread. Of this I am sure.

Sometimes malaria got boys in my tent, in my own little family. When that happened, it was up to the rest of us in the family to carry the dead body to the burial place. I lost many friends in this way.

Life may have been hard, but we were happy. Yes, boys died and food was difficult to come by, but at least no one was shooting at us. We only ate one meal a day, but for me, coming into the camp at the age of six, I accepted this as normal. I never thought that life was unfair because I had to eat garbage. Instead, I looked at the scraps of food from the dump as a blessing. Not all the boys in the camp could do this. I knew some who chose to feel sorry for themselves, who complained constantly about their lot in life. What is the point of such complaining? After all the whining and complaining is over, you still live in a refugee camp. All the complaining in the world will not make your life any better. Instead, you must choose to make the best of whatever the situation in which you find yourself, even in a place like Kakuma.

I found it easier to maintain a positive attitude when I stayed busy. My friends and I stayed busy playing soccer. Someone made a ball by tying together rags from the dump. It did not bounce like a real soccer ball, but at least we never had to worry about it running out of air.

Nearly every boy in Kakuma played soccer. I loved the game. On the field I lived up to my name, which meant "fast." I weaved through lines of defenders so quickly no one could stop me. I became one of the best scorers in the camp. Perhaps I was too good. The other boys came up to me and complained, "Lopepe, you never pass the ball to your team-mates." I did not listen. After all, the point of soccer is to score more goals than the other team, not to pass the ball. I kept playing the way I always had. Eventually the other boys had enough. One day I walked out on the soccer field and one of the older boys who ran the games told me, "From now on you are the goalkeeper."

At first I hated being the goalkeeper. You cannot score from the back side of the field, and I love scoring goals. But what could I do? Instead of sulking, I told myself, Okay, you are now the goalkeeper. Make yourself the best goalkeeper in all of Kenya. And I did. By this time I was eleven or twelve years old, no longer one of the youngest boys in the camp. I still was not big, but I was fast in the goal. I blocked anything and everything.

Kakuma grew larger and larger. Every day we heard the distinctive sound of army trucks pulling up to the gate, delivering more refugees. Just as when I arrived, boys far outnumbered adults and families among the new arrivals. These boys crowded onto the soccer field, making it impossible to play. To solve this problem, the older boys came up with a plan. Before anyone could set foot on the soccer field, they first had to run one lap around the camp. The faster you finished your lap, the sooner you got to play soccer. Kakuma did not have a fence around it, but the perimeter was very clearly defined. One lap around the outside of all the tents from all the sections from all the tribes and nationalities equaled thirty kilometers—that is, eighteen miles. We ran without shoes and without extra water in the hot Kenyan desert.

While that may sound like torture to many people, to me, running those thirty kilometers allowed me to escape the realities of life in the camp. When I ran, I did not think about my empty stomach or how I ended up in this place. I could not control much in my life. The UN dictated when food was delivered, when the water spigots were turned on, even when they dumped their garbage for us to eat. But when I ran, I was in control of my life. I ran for me. None of us had shoes, yet running barefoot connected me to the ground under my feet. It was as though the path under my feet and I became one.

Running became my therapy, but I ran fast because I loved soccer. The faster I finished my lap, the more soccer I got to play. When I finished my one lap around the camp, I didn't take a water break. I didn't want to waste time going over to the water station when I could be playing ball. Camels drink once and go on for weeks, and so could I. I was a soccer camel.

When I was not running around the camp or playing soccer, I went to school. Every weekday morning from eight until noon, I attended UN-sponsored classes. We did not have a classroom. Instead, we met under a large canvas tent workers put up to protect students from the sun. The school also did not supply textbooks. We sang most of our lessons. A few lucky boys had books they'd brought with them to the camp, but they were few and far between. In place of books, I used to sit under the stars and remember the stories my mother told me as a little boy. I knew that somewhere, she was under the same sky. The thought made me feel connected to her somehow.

We also did not have paper and pencils. A few boys did—those who were sponsored by someone on the other side of the world. I was not so lucky. I used to stare at those writing with a real pen and think, *Oh, to be so rich as to have a pen in my pocket. Someday, that will be me.* In the meantime, I wrote my lessons in the dirt with a stick. The teacher walked between the rows of boys, checking our work. If I got the problem wrong or if I wrote my letters incorrectly, the teacher smacked me with a stick. "Why did you write that letter that way?" the teacher would say. The beatings motivated me to do my best. I did not enjoy getting smacked with a stick.

On Sunday we went to church instead of school. It was my favorite day of the week. Everything was good on Sundays. I didn't have to think about food or anything else. Instead, I lost myself singing praises to God. I knew He was there with me. I never, ever doubted that fact for a moment.

And God was with me for a very long time in Kakuma. I did not stay six years old very long. Before I knew it, I was one of the older boys in the camp. Instead of having teenage friends look after me, I took on that role with the younger ones. I never questioned that role or anything else about life in Kakuma. That was just the way things were in the camp—the way life was, and the way it would always be. I never expected anything more.

SIX

From Lopepe to Joseph

I do not remember the day I came to the realization that my parents were dead. I did not wake up one morning crying, "Oh no! My mother and father are gone. What will I ever do?" During my imprisonment in the rebel camp, I dreamed nonstop about going home. When my angels came to me, they told me I was going to see my mother again. Knowing she was waiting for me carried me through the savannah when my feet left a trail of blood with every step. I did not feel the thorn bushes tearing at my legs because I knew I was on my way home.

But our path did not take us home. It took us to Kenya and Kakuma, a place filled with boys like me, boys without homes, without mothers or fathers. Every day I wondered if today might be the day my parents would come and take me home. Surely they must be out there somewhere, searching for me anywhere and everywhere. Their search had to bring them to Kakuma. Once they walked through the gates, I would be on my way home.

Days turned into weeks, but they never walked through the gates.

"Why don't they come?" I asked over and over to anyone who would listen during my first weeks in the camp. Tears flowed. "If they are looking for me, why can't they find me?"

"You can't think like that, Lopepe," a friend finally answered. I tried to look away and ignore him, but he got right in my face.

"Stop it, Lopepe. *Stop!* You see that boy over there?" He pointed to a boy we all knew about. Like me, he was one of the younger ones. Unlike me, he was not going to survive much longer. He rarely left his tent. All day every day he sat in his tent rocking, rocking, rocking, his mind slowly slipping away. "You cannot sit and wish for something that is never going to happen, or you will lose your mind. No, you must focus on here and now. Do your chores. Go to school. Keep your mind busy. The past is gone. It will not come back. You must live in this day."

"But . . ." I said, tears welling up in my eyes.

"No buts," he said. "This is the life you now have. You must accept it and go forward or you will end up like that other boy." He then smiled at me, which seemed oddly out of place. "You can do this, my friend. I know you can. You are strong." My friend patted me on the back and left to go play soccer.

I sat and stared at the rocking boy for a very long time. There were others like him in Kakuma, boys who cried for home day and night. Eventually, malaria always got these boys. I did not want to suffer such a fate. The rocking boy looked over at me, his eyes filled with sadness. *What will it be, Lopepe?* I asked myself. The answer was easy. I jumped up, ran out of the tent, and chased after my friend to the soccer field.

My homesickness did not immediately stop, but it changed. The moment I ran over to the soccer field, I knew my parents were never going to come and rescue me. I would not see my home again.

Once I made peace with the fact that I would never go home again, the next step came quite naturally. I did not have a home any longer, and for all practical purposes, I no longer had a mother or father. That made me an orphan. How could I be an orphan if my parents still lived? My mind completed the thought: *My parents have to be dead.* I knew they were. I knew it just as surely as I knew the sun came up in the east and went down in the west.

My parents were gone, but I remained. In many ways, I was the same boy I was in Kimotong. Back home, I pestered my mother and father for chores. In Kakuma, I did not have to ask what to do. We all had specific tasks we had to do every day. "You will stand in line for water every morning, Lopepe," I was told as a boy handed me a five-gallon jerrican.

"Show me where to go and I will do it," I said. The UN piped in water for the camp. The water station consisted of four spigots where we filled up our cans. However, four spigots aren't very many for the thousands who lived in the camp. My first couple of years in Kakuma, I had to wake up in the middle of the night, grab my can, and go wait in line. At six, I was too small to carry the filled bucket back to the tent. One of the older boys came and got it. I did not like having to hand my jerrican over to someone else. "Someday," I told myself, "I will be big enough to carry the can back myself."

When I was little, as soon as my chores were over, I went out and played hide-and-seek with my friends. When the rains came and the creek filled up with water, my buddies and I swam until our arms gave out. Then we built little houses in the sand along the shore. We played house with those sandcastles, just like we did in Kimotong.

By my fifth or sixth year in the camp, I did not have time for games, although I still played soccer. In Kakuma soccer is not a game but a way of life. The rest of the time, I took on more and more responsibilities. I was in charge of the ration cards for all the boys in our tent. To make sure no one lost his card, I kept them all together in a safe place. I also calculated our daily rations. The UN handed out food once a month. I had to make the grain they gave us last until the next distribution. It was up to me to take out just the right amount for each meal. If I miscalculated, we would go hungry. I made sure I never miscalculated. Every Christmas and Easter the UN also gave us a chicken, one for each tent. One chicken is not very much meat for ten hungry boys. Therefore, to make it stretch, we cooked it in a soup. Not everyone actually got a piece of meat. But by making it into a soup, we all got a taste of chicken. I made sure of that.

The more responsibilities I took on, the more I wanted. I loved to work. I enjoyed taking care of the younger boys. We had to look out for one another to survive, and survival was the name of the game in the camp. But I wanted to thrive, not just survive. I looked for ways to do more for my family of boys. One of the many relief agencies who came in and out of Kakuma handed out some vegetable seeds. I helped plant a garden next to our house, and I carried the water to each little plant to keep it from dying in the desert sun.

Slowly but surely, I was becoming a different boy. The way I saw life in the camp evolved, as did the way I viewed church and my relationship with God. When I was a little boy, going to church and singing praises to God was enough for me. I loved church, and I loved to sing. The boys in the camp became an informal choir. We passed the time singing and singing and singing. As a little boy, I sang in the tenor section. When I got older, I tried to make my voice deep enough to move to the bass section. The priest listened to me sing a note or two and put me back with the tenors.

The longer I was in Kakuma, the more central to my life church became. It was my doorway out of the refugee camp and into a wider world. I heard news from the outside there. It was also our post office. But the best part was the worship. When I was at church, I did not think about hunger or malaria or any of the hardships of the camp. I didn't pray that God would provide for me in the camp. I was just trying to survive, and going to church was a part of that survival.

A turning point for me came a few weeks before Christmas when the priest announced confirmation classes were to begin the following week. "A baptism service will follow on Christmas Eve for those who completed the class and are serious about a relationship with God," he said. His words touched me deep in my soul. I knew this was something I must do. Perhaps I was prompted by my growing up in so many other ways. I had taken on more responsibility in the camp and in my family. Now was the time for me to take responsibility in my relationship with God as well. I knew He had always been with me. Now was the time for a deeper relationship with Him.

The next week when the first class started, I was there. Again, I did not have a Bible and no one in the class had any kind of book to read. Instead, the priest taught us from the Bible orally. I was used to this. My parents taught me the Bible the same way, and I also learned in school without books. In my culture in Sudan, we handed down our most important stories by word of mouth when we did not have a written language. Learning this way came naturally for me.

Over the three or four weeks leading up to Christmas, the priest taught us many Bible stories. More than that, He taught us how to be close to God. That's what I wanted. I did not have an earthly mother or father any longer. I wanted to have that Father relationship with God.

The weeks of classes passed quickly. Christmas Eve service came. The priest went through the regular Christmas Eve mass. I was nervous. Very nervous. I loved Christmas. We did not exchange gifts or do any of the traditions Americans celebrate. I loved Christmas because of the meaning of the day. Here we were, Christmas Eve, sitting in church, remembering the birth of our Savior. I looked up at the night sky and imagined what it would have been like to be one of the shepherds out in the field on a night very much like this one. They were minding their own business when angels appeared telling them about the birth of Jesus. I was not waiting for an angel to appear on this night. Instead I was listening for the priest to call on me and the other boys who were to be baptized that night.

Finally he did. "Okay, boys," he said. "It is time."

I looked around at my friends and swallowed hard. I thought back to my classes and tried to remember what I was supposed to say and when I was supposed to say it. My mind went blank. About twenty of us filed up to the front and formed a semicircle around the altar. One of the attendants walked down the line, handing candles to each of us. I grasped my candle, thinking, but I still could not remember. I knew what was in my heart. I was standing here, taking my stand for God. Now everyone in the camp knew that I had made up my mind to follow Jesus. I was ready to take up my cross and follow Him, but I was not sure what I was supposed to say when the priest came to me and asked me the appointed question. *What is he going to ask?* I was too nervous to remember.

The church was dark except for the candles on the altar. One of the workers lit the boy's candle on the far right side. He dipped his candle down and lit the candle of the next boy, who lit the next one, who lit the next one, and on around the circle. I was just to the left of the middle. When the flame came to me, I bent my candle over and carefully lit it. I held my breath just a little as I turned to the boy next to me. The last thing I wanted to do was accidentally blow out my candle and mess up the night for everyone.

Once all the candles were lit, the priest came up. I looked to my right, then to my left. The candlelight lit up the faces of my friends, like the faces of angels. The priest walked up to the boy on the far right side. Another worker walked beside him, carrying water and oil. My heart pounded in my ears. I'd thought about this night for a while and what it meant. For this to take place on Christmas Eve made it even more meaningful for me. What better time to express my faith in Jesus than on His birthday?

The priest came closer. He stopped at a boy a couple down from me. I could not quite hear what he said. *What are you supposed to say, Lopepe?* I could not remember, but suddenly I did not care. Whatever he asked me, I would tell him what was in my heart.

He stopped at the boy just to my right. Out of the corner of my eye, I saw the priest reach down into one container, touch the boy's head, then reach into the other container and do the same.

Then the priest stepped over to me.

My candle lit his face. He smiled. I did my best to smile back. His right hand came up to my forehead. He traced the sign of the cross on me with oil. Without asking any questions, he baptized me and said, "You are now Joseph, and I baptize you in the name of the Father, the Son, and the Holy Spirit."

It is hard to describe what came over me in that moment. Second Corinthians 5:17 says that if anyone is in Christ he is a new creation. All the old things have passed away and everything is made new. That verse came true for me that night. I was a new boy with a new name. In the Bible, Jesus often changed the names of His disciples. He changed Simon's name to Peter and Saul's name to Paul. Now He changed my name from Lopepe to Joseph.

I stood in the night air, staring at my candle, thinking about what I knew of Joseph in the Bible. There are two well-known Josephs. One is the father of Jesus, a hard-working man who made a living as a carpenter. The other is found in the book of Genesis. Like me, he was taken from his home when he was young. He was carried away to Egypt as a slave. Later, he was thrown into prison even though he had done nothing wrong. Yet, no matter what happened to him, God was always with him. Joseph did not sit around feeling sorry for himself. Instead, he went to work. When he was a slave, he worked so hard and proved himself so trustworthy, that his owner put his entire household under Joseph's care. After he was thrown into prison, the chief jailer did the same thing. He knew Joseph was a hard worker who always kept his word.

Standing in front of the altar, oil in the shape of a cross glistening on my forehead, my head wet from my baptism, I made up my mind that I wanted to live up to my new name. Joseph was not just any name to me. It was the name God had picked out for me in eternity past.

This is who I am. I am Joseph, a follower of Jesus, trustworthy and hardworking. I am no longer a lost boy. I am a brand-new man.

SEVEN

A New Dream

A buzz rose in the camp in the late summer of 2000. Everyone talked about a strange new thing. A word flew around the camp, a word I had never heard before. During school, it was the hot topic. Running my lap around the camp, I heard more about it. Out on the soccer field, boys went on and on about it like they were some kind of experts on this thing called the Olympics.

"Are you excited about the Olympics, Lopepe?" someone asked me.

"Sure," I said, not wanting to sound ignorant. "Isn't everyone?"

"I know I am," the kid said and ran off.

I didn't get it. I'd lived in the camp for over nine years, about as long as anyone, but I'd never heard of this Olympics thing before. I have no idea how anyone else ever heard of the Olympics, but that was pretty much business as usual in Kakuma. Some kid heard a news bit from outside the camp while hanging out near the UN compound; he told another kid, who told another, and in less time than it takes an American teenager to send a text message to all his contacts, the news was all over the camp. No one had to understand what was going on to get excited about it. The Olympics gave us something new to talk about and broke up the monotony of the daily routine in Kakuma.

Other boys were all excited about the Olympics, but I found my own way to break up the routine of the camp. During one of my pre-soccer thirty kilometer runs, I noticed a farm not far from the camp. I'd seen the farm for years, but I never really noticed it until now. The farmer had a car, which made him a rich man in this part of Kenya. But that's not what caught my eye. The grass around his house grew tall even though he had a cow nearby. His tall grass gave me an idea.

I trotted over to the farmer's house and introduced myself. "I would like to help you," I said.

The farmer gave me a look that said, *You. What can you possibly do for me?*

"I am a hard worker," I said. "I used to help take care of my father's two hundred cattle back home. I can take care of your cow and cut your grass."

"I don't pay people to do things I can do myself," he said.

"I don't need much," I said. "If I do a good job, just give me whatever you think is right. If I don't, don't give me anything." For me, this was about more than money. I needed to find something to do, something productive. I was sick of Tuesday trash day being the highlight of my life. I needed to work.

The man thought for a moment. "Okay, you can take care of the cow and cut the grass starting tomorrow morning."

"I will be here," I said. I went back and finished my lap around the camp, then joined in the soccer game.

Working outside the camp was against the rules, so I kept my job to myself. But that didn't stop me from working as hard as I could. After a few days the farmer came out to where I was working. "Here," he said and held out his hand. "This is for you."

He dropped a five shilling coin into my hand. I wrapped my hand tight around it. "*Asante Sana,*" I said, which means "thank you" in Swahili.

"*Karibu,*" he said and walked away. That is, "you're welcome."

I shoved the coin into my pocket and went back to work. Thoughts of all I could buy with my newfound fortune raced through my mind. The camp had an underground economy where you could buy bread or candy or paper and pencils or anything your heart may desire. All those things looked so good when I didn't have any money. But now that I did, they didn't look quite as attractive. By the time I returned to my tent, I'd decided to hold onto the coin for a while. I liked the weight of it in my pocket. Since this was basically the first money I'd ever had, I was in no hurry to turn loose of it.

All the while, Olympics buzz kept building in the camp. One day while playing soccer, a friend came up to me. "Do you want to go watch the Olympics with us tonight?"

"Okay," I said, unsure of what I was getting myself into. "Who's going?"

"A bunch of us," he said. He started rattling off names, which was not necessary.

"Sure, sure," I cut him off. "I'm in. Where do we watch these Olympics?"

"We found a place. A rich guy said we can watch them at his house."

Later that afternoon, I joined a group of fifteen guys and we took off walking to go see these Olympics. I still had no idea what they might be. I knew it had something to do with sports, and since soccer was the only real sport I knew anything about, I thought it might have something to do with soccer. However, I did not dare ask more questions and make myself out as the only boy in the entire camp who did not know what the Olympics were.

We walked five miles, out beyond the edge of the camp. I was very surprised when we stopped at the home of the farmer for whom I worked. One of the boys knocked on the door. The farmer opened the door with a suspicious look on his face. He looked our group up and down. "Okay," he said, "you can come in and watch the Olympics, but don't touch anything. And don't sit on my furniture." He opened the door wider and then said, "It will cost you five shillings apiece."

My heart sank when I heard that. The other boys all pulled out their money without a moment's hesitation. I reached into my pocket and felt that wonderful coin. I had such plans for it. The other boys had already gone inside when I finally took the money out of my pocket. I started to tell the man, "Forget it," and leave, but I did not want to walk the five miles back to my tent all by myself. And I really wanted to find out what made this thing called the Olympics so special that these boys would hand over their hard-earned money so quickly.

The man looked at me. "Well?" he said.

I dropped the coin in his hand and walked inside.

Locals filled the farmer's living room. Every piece of furniture had someone on it.

"You boys are too dirty to sit on the sofa. There, sit on the floor," the farmer said. We did as we were told.

I looked around the living room. The Olympics was not what I expected. Apparently it consisted of a box with wires running out the back of it. The wires were connected to a car battery. *This is the Olympics? I thought. What is so special about this?*

The farmer walked over and flipped a switch on the front of the box. Black, white, and gray images flickered to life. The box was not the Olympics. It was something else I'd heard about but never seen: a television.

The farmer switched the channel and the Olympics came on the screen. The boys all cheered. I cheered with them. Unfortunately, soccer players did not run out onto the screen. Instead, the athletes stayed outside the big field in the middle, on a little road with white lines drawn on it. They took their places behind a white line. A man held up a gun. It fired. The guys on the screen took off running. Thousands upon thousands of people filled the stands around the track. As the men ran, the people screamed and carried on. When the winner crossed the finish line, the crowd cheered even louder.

Watching people run on television was a revelation for me. Never before had I thought of running as a sport. When I ran, I did not think about conditions in the camp or the hunger in my belly. Running was my therapy, my release, my escape from the world around me.

Yet in the Olympics, running was a sport. And judging by the number of people in the stands, it was a popular sport. I was mesmerized by it. This was fascinating.

Then came the highlight of the night for me. Runners took their places for a very important race. The announcers talked about one runner in particular, a man named Michael Johnson. I did not know it at the time, but this race was the 400-meter dash, or one lap around the track in a full sprint. Michael Johnson was both the defending Olympic champion and the world record holder in the event. I did not know that at the time. Nor did I know that this was to be his final race, the capstone to one of the most successful track careers of all time. All I knew was the camera focused primarily on one man, a man with skin the color of mine. Across his chest were three letters: USA. He was about to change my life.

The runners took their mark. The gun sounded. Michael Johnson took off. He ran with a very distinctive style: head up, back straight, everything about him screamed confidence. Watching him run on the small, black-and-white television hooked up to a car battery in a remote corner of Kenya, he did not appear to be moving all that fast. *I can run like that. I know that I can.*

Michael Johnson flew around the track. He ran through the string at the end before anyone else. The announcers said he'd just won the gold medal. I was not sure what that was. He took a flag from someone in the crowd, a flag with stars and stripes on it. He wrapped himself in that flag with pride; then he held it up and ran a victory lap with it. I knew this was a very, very special moment.

Then something happened that astounded me. The top three runners took their places on a small platform. A man came up and placed their medals around their necks. Music began to play, and flags rose up from behind the men. As the music played and the flags went up in the air, Michael Johnson did something African men never do: he wept openly and without shame. I shook my head in disbelief and leaned closer to the screen. *Why was he crying?* I wondered. How can a man like this, a man who just won an Olympic gold medal, show such emotion? In my culture, such a display was a sign of weakness. Yet Michael Johnson had just proven his strength and confidence to the world. Why, then, did he cry?

These thoughts had barely had time to bounce into my brain before the farmer stepped over to the television. He flipped the switch. The black, white, and gray images disappeared. "Five more shillings," he said. The local Kenyans and my friends dug in their pockets. Everyone had more money except me. When the farmer came to me with his hand held out, I shrugged my shoulders. "Sorry, kid," he said. "No money, no Olympics."

"Okay," I said. My friends all looked at me with sad expressions on their faces. However, no one dug down and paid five shillings for me. That was fine. I smiled. "I'll see you guys back at camp."

Outside, night had fallen. The stars shone overhead, bright and beautiful. I started back on that long, familiar walk toward my tent. The trail we ran every day came close to the farmer's house. Even in the dark, I knew where I was and how to get back to where I needed to go. I walked along in the night, staring up at the night sky. The image of Michael Johnson standing on that platform, the letters *USA* across his chest, weeping openly and without shame, flashed through my head. For a man to react to winning a race in such a manner told me that this had been more than a race. Those letters on his chest and the flag he carried around the track, they had to be the key. Clearly, he was not just running for himself. The gold medal by itself was not enough to bring a real man to tears. No, this man, this man with skin like mine, ran for something bigger than himself. That had to be why he wept.

I walked through the night, these thoughts dancing in my head. Suddenly, an idea hatched in my brain, an idea that should have struck me as ridiculous, but it did not. To me, this idea made perfect sense. In my mind's eye I watched Michael Johnson run his race over and over again and I knew that someday, I, too, would run in the Olympics. I did not know how, but I knew I would. I now had a dream that changed the course of my life: I would be an Olympian. Moreover, I wanted to run with those same three letters across my chest: USA. I wanted to be like Michael Johnson.

The next day came just like every day before in Kakuma. I went off to school in the morning, working out my lessons with a stick in the sand. At noon, school let out, which meant it was now time to run one lap around the camp, then spend the rest of the day on the soccer field. The day may have been like every day before, but I was now different. I took off running my thirty kilometer lap, but my mind was not on soccer. With every step, I saw Michael Johnson; I saw the Olympics; I saw myself running for the USA.

The scenery flying past me on my run looked different as well. From the day I arrived in Kakuma, the camp defined my world. I thought I would always live here, because I never saw anyone leave. The camp kept growing bigger and bigger as more and more refugees flooded in from a never-ending civil war. Life revolved around Tuesday trash day and a brief escape from reality during church on Sundays. That's all there was, and all there ever would be.

Not anymore. I knew a life existed for me beyond the perimeter of Kakuma. God Himself had brought me to Kakuma. I always thought He must have had a reason for bringing me here. Now I had it. Now I knew where my destiny lay. Michael Johnson opened a wider world to me. By God's grace, I would get there.

EIGHT

Writing for My Life

The United States of America has decided to allow a limited number of you boys to leave Kakuma and go to America," the priest announced one October Sunday less than two months after I watched Michael Johnson run in the Olympics. The priest might as well have said Jesus had thrown open the doors of heaven to us. From where I lived, the only difference between America and heaven was that I had to die to go to heaven.

I knew all about America—at least I thought I did. The boys in the camp talked about America with the same degree of authority they used when discussing the Olympics. "Everyone eats as much food as they want," boys said. "Anyone in America can get any job they want," I heard. "That's the place where all your dreams come true."

The occasional sight of an American in our camp only confirmed everything we thought we knew. Every American who visited the camp stood tall and clean and well fed and white and pure. We boys in the camp looked and smelled bad because we had no place to bathe. But

Americans, they were white just like the pictures of Jesus I'd seen. That's why I thought Americans must be close to God, and America must be like heaven. Every boy in the camp dreamed of going to America some-day, but we knew that was one dream that had no chance of coming true.

Until now.

A real live American stood up to fill us in on the details. "Thirty-five hundred boys from Kakuma will be allowed to move to the United States permanently," he said in English, which was translated into Swahili by one of the camp directors. "Anyone can apply to be one of the thirty-five hundred. You must write an essay in English that tells your story. We will accept essays for the next three weeks, but obviously, the sooner you turn yours in, the better. Once we receive your essays, we will read through them and make our selections."

"You can bring your essays here to the church," the priest added. "We will send them on to the American embassy."

We sang a final song. Church let out. We boys went nuts. "America... America . . . America . . ." Everyone started talking about America. Questions flew around the room. Everyone asked one another the same things: "Did the *mzungu* [white man] say what I thought he said?" "How did they find out about us in America?" "Do you think this is real?" "Who will get to go?" Every boy wanted to be one of the thirty-five hun-dred. If they were like me, they felt they *had* to be one of the thirty-five hundred.

Thirty-five hundred. The number sounded so high yet so small at the same time. When I ran my lap around the camp each day, there were boys as far as the eye could see. I never thought of trying to count them all, but I knew thirty-five hundred was a drop in the bucket compared to so many lost boys. And I'd heard other boys' stories. Everyone had lived through hell. Many of these boys had lived through hell far longer than me. You couldn't even call a lot of them boys anymore.

Civil war broke out in Sudan in 1983. The first group of lost boys escaped in a large group a short time later. They went to a refugee camp in Ethiopia. However, when the government changed there, the boys had to flee for their lives once again. Perhaps as many as a thousand died on the journey. Many drowned or were eaten by crocodiles when they crossed the Gilo River from Ethiopia into Kenya. The rest of the lost boys were like me, boys who escaped Sudan as the war went on and on and on. Some had been kidnapped and escaped. Others fled when their villages were destroyed by bombs or soldiers. All of us had suffered incredible hardship. How could the United States choose which of us to give new lives, and which to leave behind to live forever in Kakuma?

"So, Lopez," a friend said, calling me by the nickname the boys gave me in Kakuma, "are you going to write an essay?"

"Of course," I said. "Isn't everyone?"

"I don't know English well enough to write a whole essay. Do you?"

I shrugged my shoulders and smiled. "I won't let a little thing like that get in my way."

And I didn't.

The moment the church service ended, I went back to my tent to pray. "Father, I cannot write anything that stands out from all the other boys in this camp. But I trust You. If You want me in America, I know You will lift up my essay and make it stand out. You will take me to America, not this essay."

Outside my tent, boys ran and played like any other day, only today they talked about America instead of the Olympics or soccer. I did not have time to join in. I wanted to turn in my essay as soon as possible, before the thirty-five hundred spots filled up. *But what do I say?* I wondered. The man said we were to tell our story. My story began at church. Suddenly it occurred to me that it was not a coincidence that I heard of this opportunity to go to America while at church. I could have heard it anywhere. The *mzungu* might have come to our school on Monday and announced it there. Instead he came on Sunday, to church, to my church. Nearly ten years earlier I went to church one Sunday expecting to worship God, but I ended up in a prison camp. Now God had opened a door to America during church. "God, this has to be part of Your plan," I prayed.

Before I could start writing, I had to come up with a pencil and paper. Even after ten years in Kakuma, I still did my school lessons in the dirt with a stick. Pencil and paper were hard to find for school, but not for this essay. Most of the boys in my section of the camp knew me. We all looked out for one another. As soon as word got out that I needed pencil and paper, one of the sponsored boys offered me both.

Back in my tent, I sat down and composed my thoughts. "Ten years ago, I woke up early to go to church with my mother and father," I wrote in Swahili. "We were praying when trucks filled with soldiers came up. The soldiers pointed guns at us. They ordered us to lie down on the ground. I lay down next to my mother. She wrapped her arm around me. A soldier pulled her arm away and picked me up. He threw me in the back of a truck along with all the other boys and girls from my village. They took us to a prison camp."

Memories rushed back. I remembered details of the day I was taken that I had not thought about for a very long time. It was as though I was back there, reliving the whole thing again. I saw the trucks. I heard the soldiers. I felt the hot truck bed on my bare legs.

"The soldiers blindfolded me in the back of the truck and threw me to the ground. They put my hand on the back of another boy. They marched us in a line. They beat many of the boys. I heard them scream in pain. The line stopped. Someone pulled the blindfold off my face. He pushed me into a hut filled with boys." I wrote about the smell and how boys died every day.

"Three boys and I escaped through a hole in the fence one night." I remembered how the door did not squeak and how the soldiers guarding us did not notice us crawling across the compound. "We crawled through the fence. Then we started running. We ran for our lives for three days across the desert." The more I wrote, the more details I remembered. I could not write down everything that happened. I only had one sheet of paper, and I was supposed to write an essay, not a book. Yet I somehow knew exactly what to include and what details to leave out.

I kept writing and writing and writing. Words spilled across the page. I was not nervous. I did not wonder what the Americans would think of my story or whether they would find it strong enough to select me as one of the thirty-five hundred. Sitting in my tent, paper and pencil in hand, I did not write my story for the Americans. This essay was a prayer I wrote for God alone, a prayer I hoped He would answer.

Once I finished writing my story in Swahili, I read it over and then read it over again. I changed a few things here and there, but not very much. I would like to say the first draft was perfect, but I had no way of knowing if it was any good. This was my story, in my voice. Unfortunately, my voice only came out in Swahili. The Americans did not want Swahili. They would only accept English. I knew I could not translate my essay by myself.

I went to my friends, my family of boys who lived with me in my tent. "Guys, I need some help," I said. Over the next few days, writing for my life became a community project.

My friends gathered around me while I sat at a makeshift table. I laid out a brand-new sheet of paper. A friend loaned me a pen with which to write in English. I did not want to turn in a scribbled mess. This essay had to look as good as it sounded. The former was much easier than the latter.

"Okay, Lopez, what do you have?" one asked.

"*Tafadhali Mungu ni saidye.*"

"Do you know how to say that in English?"

"I think," I said. I took out my pen. "Please, God, help me," I wrote. "What's next?"

"*Wakati nilikuwa mtoto mdogo, wajeishi walikuja wa kanisa yetu boma ya Kimotong nchi yetu wa Sudani. Wanabeba bunduki kubwa.*" I stared at it for a moment. "I have no idea how to put this into English," I said.

One of the boys pointed at the first sentence. "I have it. When I was child little, soldiers came," he said in English. Then in Swahili, "Uh, what's the next word?"

"Village," another said in English.

"How do you spell that?" I asked.

"V-i-l-l-a-g-e"

I hesitated.

"It looks like this," he said, and drew a *v* in the dirt with his hand.

"Right," I said. Carefully, I penned the English words as best I could. "Please, God, help me. When I was child little, soldiers came church ours village Kimotong my country Sudan."

"*Kuchukwa watoto wadogo kufundishya jinzi wa wajeishi. Mimi ni lukua na wao,*" became, "Carry with them guns big. Take children young teach become a soldier. I am among them . . . We went to fence. We ran through bush dark three days . . ."

Our community English project left much to be desired, but it was the best we could do. Over the next few hours my friends called out English words from my Swahili. More than once we debated a word for a while before landing on the best translation. It seems very funny to me now to think that I could not even read the essay I was writing. I had no idea what most of the English words meant, but I trusted my family.

After we finished my essay, we helped other boys turn their Swahili into English as they wrote for their lives too. "Someday," I said, "we will all be in America, with jobs and food, and it will be great." The thought made us work that much harder to perfect our essays. This was our chance at freedom, our only chance. "Oh God, hear my prayer," I prayed. "Let my cry come to You."

I took my essay to church the next Sunday. "To You, God," I prayed as I dropped it in the bin near the front of the church as an offering. If all the boys were like me, God received a lot of offerings that morning. The bin was filled to the top with hundreds of essays. I walked back into the crowd and found a seat on one of the homemade benches. The music began. We stood to sing, but my mind was not on the songs. I stared at the bin. With so many desperate boys from which to choose, how would the Americans decide who goes and who stays behind? I was glad I did not have to make that decision. If it were up to me, every boy in the camp would be on the next bus to America.

The music stopped. The priest delivered his sermon. I could not listen. The bin of essays had my full and undivided attention. "It is up to You, God," I prayed. "You will decide." Yes, it was up to Him, not the Americans. God would indeed decide what was best for me. He had brought me to Kakuma with my three angels. He must have a plan for when and how I was to leave. Knowing God was in control was the only thing that allowed me to stop fixating on the bin and to go back to my tent as church ended. I knew I wrote the best essay I could possibly write. My friends and I translated it into English as best we could. I could do nothing more. The rest was up to God.

Sunday came again. I went to church. We sang. The priest preached. At the end of the service he read a list of boys who had turned in essays. He did not say which boys would get to go to America.

More Sundays came and went. Weeks had gone by since I dropped my essay in the bin, but still no word from the Americans. "They never intended to let us leave," a boy said. "Do you know what people out there call us?"

I shook my head.

"Lost boys of Sudan. No one thinks about us. No one cares about lost boys."

I did not argue the point. What good would it do?

Christmas approached, my favorite time of the year. I made plans for the chicken our tent would soon receive. My heart wasn't in it. I found it hard to get excited about a chicken while waiting to be told if I'd get to live in America.

The UN passed out the Christmas chickens. We had our feast and then went to church for Christmas, Jesus' birthday, the day I became Joseph, the worker, the new man. I walked into our church. Something was different. The *mzungu* was back. My heart raced. He announced, "Please come forward when I read your name."

He called the first name. A boy went up front. They handed him an envelope. *What does that mean? What is inside the envelope? Is it good news or bad?*

More names were called. More boys went forward. More envelopes were handed out. I waited, nervous and excited. Every time the *mzungu* opened his mouth, my heart skipped a beat. *Will my name be next?* He opened his mouth. I held my breath. "Joseph Lopepe Lomong," he said. I leaped out of my seat. I couldn't believe my head missed the ceiling, I jumped so high. My friends clapped and patted me on the back, congratulating me. I tried to stay calm. I strolled up to the front. A worker placed a large, white envelope in my hands. I went back to my seat, my heart pounding.

"Open it," a friend said.

"What does it say?" said another.

"You're going to America," someone said.

"You're not going to America," someone else said.

"Open it, Lopez!" A friend nudged me.

I clutched the envelope tightly. I could not open it in front of so many people. If it were bad news, I knew I could not control my emotions. And if it were good news . . . oh, the emotions would flow as well.

The last name was called. Church let out. Excited boys with envelopes danced out; dejected boys without envelopes could hardly make their feet work. I ran out to a place where I could be alone. I pulled out the envelope. Carefully, I slid a finger under the flap. I pulled out a very official-looking document. I closed my eyes, said a quick prayer, and breathed in deep. *Okay, this is it. America or Kakuma: which will it be?* I opened my eyes to read my fate.

"What?" I said. The entire thing was written in English! I could not read a single word except my name.

I walked back to the church. One of my friends who could read and speak English well was still there. "Can you tell me what this says?" I asked.

He took one look and broke out in a huge grin.

"Congratulations, Lopez. You are going to America!"

NINE

No Good-Byes

I heard the airplane before I saw it. I was in my tent with my friends, talking about America, when we heard the drone of its propellers. "This is it!" I yelled. I jumped up, grabbed the white envelope I received at church a week earlier, and took off running toward the airfield in the middle of the camp. Every boy in my tent was right on my heels. I and a couple of my friends had been told to be ready as soon as the plane landed. We were to go to Nairobi for our America interviews. I didn't know the reasons behind the interviews, but if it would get me to America, I didn't need to know the reason.

"I'm going to beat you there," a boy called as he tried to run past me.

I laughed and kicked it into another gear. When you live in a camp full of boys, everything becomes a competition.

The plane rolled to a stop, its propellers still spinning. I ran into the crowd of boys who lined the sides of the airstrip. A *mzungu* in a ball cap held up a clipboard. "When I call your name, step up and get on the plane." Unlike waiting for the *mzungu* handing out the white envelopes at church, I knew my name was on this list. He went through several names before calling out, "Joseph Lopepe Lomong."

I jumped up and down, a huge grin on my face, waving the envelope over my head. "Here! Here!" I said.

"Get on up here," the *mzungu* said.

I pushed my way through the crowd. All my friends were as happy for me as I was for myself. Guys I did not know cheered and clapped. "I'll see you guys after my interviews," I said to one of the boys from my tent.

"Tell me what it's like," he said. "I'm going myself one day."

"We're all going to go soon!" I called back as I ran up to the plane. The *mzungu* took my envelope, gave it a quick once-over, and then handed it back to me. "Find a seat," he said as he motioned me up the stairs that led up into the back of the plane. A couple of boys from my tent whose names had been called were already seated. They both gave me a thumbs-up. You've never seen a happier bunch of boys.

I sat down. The airplane filled up. A nice lady came over and showed me how to buckle my seat belt. I'd never ridden in anything with seat belts. I'd never ridden in anything except the rebel army truck that kidnapped me and the Kenyan border guard truck that carried me to Kakuma when I was six.

The airplane propellers sprung to life. The plane slowly rolled forward. It turned twice, stopped briefly, then lunged forward very quickly. The plane gathered speed, which surprised me. I thought this was a bus. Only when the plane lifted off of the ground did I realize we were flying to Nairobi. I watched airplanes up high in the sky with my father when I was a little boy. Never in my wildest dreams did I ever imagine flying in the sky myself. I looked out the window as Kakuma grew smaller and smaller. "This is great," I said to the kid next to me, a huge grin on my face.

I did not know this was the last I would see of Kakuma. The Dominican Sisters who worked in the camp for Catholic Charities told us we were going to Nairobi for interviews and tests. (Catholic Charities was one of many aid organizations that helped lost boys go to America.) The sisters may have explained how we would stay in Nairobi until the time came to leave for America. If they did, I never made the connection between interviews, tests, shots, and orientation classes with the fact that once I stepped foot on that plane, I was never coming back to Kakuma.

If I had, my leaving would have been very different.

In Africa, family comes before everything else. Over the past ten years, the boys with whom I lived became my family. As excited as I was about going to America, the thought of leaving them behind filled me with sorrow. But I knew I had to go, if for nothing else than to find a job, earn money, and send it back to support my family stuck in Kakuma. I knew if the situation were reversed, the other boys would do the same for me. Even so, thinking about telling my family of boys good-bye made going to America very bittersweet. Unfortunately, or perhaps fortunately, I did not have to say good-bye because I did not realize this was my last day in Kakuma.

Once we landed in Nairobi, buses took us to the Boys' Center in the city of Juja.

I never counted on living there for more than a day or two. Looking back, I understand I needed to stay there for a while. Our dorm had actual toilet facilities, instead of the dry creek bed we used for a latrine in Kakuma. The toilets consisted of little more than a hole in the ground, yet that was a huge upgrade over what I'd known my entire life. Cars and people crowded the paved streets. Electric lights lit up the night, while most of the staff in the dormitory and offices spoke English. Little did I know that they were British, not American. I thought all white people were Americans. Learning the English language from Brits gave me a double accent, which complicated life for me once I arrived in the United

States. However, that did not matter in Juja. *This has to be what America is like*, I thought.

The staff in Juja gave us a crash course on life in America. My favorite class introduced me to a strange, cold, white substance. "This is snow," the instructor said as he pulled a snowball out of a cooler. "It is very cold. It falls from the sky and piles up on the ground during the winter in America." He passed the ball of snow around the classroom. I was anxious to hold it. Wow. I had never felt anything so cold in my life! How did people live in such a cold place? Then it dawned on me: *No wonder these Americans are so white. The cold and snow make them that way.* "I hope the place where I live doesn't get much of this stuff," I told one of the other boys. Little did I know God planned on sending me to one of the snowiest places in America.

Beyond learning about snow, our classes focused on things like the stripes on streets where you could cross without getting hit by a car, and money. I'm sure they tried to teach us more, but all the lessons sort of ran together—all but one.

According to my orientation classes, the one thing I needed to know about America above everything else was this: "There is no such thing as *hakuna matata* in America." I laughed the first time the instructor said this. *Hakuna matata* means "no worries." In Africa, it is more than a catchy saying. It is a way of life in the camp. Time simply does not matter. From presidents and kings and judges all the way down to boys in a refugee camp, arriving somewhere "on time" is a very foreign concept. If you say, "Be here by nine," that means, to us, "Show up sometime before noon." If you are late, *hakuna matata*—no worries. In Africa, no one expects you to show up on time, anyway.

No one, that is, except the people running things in Juja. "When you have an interview, you must not show up late. You must arrive early," I was told. "*Hukana matata* does not work in America, and it will not work here."

The instructor meant what he said. We had to arrive everywhere on time. My first interview was scheduled for nine in the morning. All the boys in my dorm had nine o'clock interviews. The workers woke us up by six thirty. We all went down to the waiting area by eight o'clock, where we did just that: we waited until our names were called. Sometimes we waited up to three hours. I wondered why I had to arrive so early, only to have to sit around and wait. I guess they were preparing us for going to the Department of Motor Vehicles in America.

During my time in Juja, I went through a series of four interviews spread over several weeks. The first interviewer asked me about my background. When we boys left the camp, we did not have birth certificates or any other paperwork. We had a name and approximate age but nothing to document either one. America will not let anyone in without lots and lots of documents. The first interview started that process. After the interview, I shuffled into a room where a man took my photograph for my official paperwork.

After the photographer was finished with me, a woman led me down the hall to a room filled with people in white coats. People in white coats in official buildings do one of two things: they either stick a needle in your arm and inject something into you, or they stick you with a needle to draw something out. This was not a room I wanted to visit again.

The second interview consisted of more basic questions about my story. This interview not only made my file of paperwork larger, but Catholic Charities used the information I gave to match me with a family in the United States. Even though I was an elder in Kakuma carrying out adult responsibilities, in the eyes of America I was still a minor. All of us lost boys talked about going to America and finding a job. I did not know it at the time, but because I was only sixteen years old, a different fate awaited me.

The third interview was much like the first two, only this time the interviewer asked me things like, "Why do you want to go to America? What is America to you? What would you do if you had to go to a different country to live?" I answered the best I could. The interviewers did all they could to put me at ease. I could not fail the interview and go back to Kakuma. I was definitely going to America, no matter what!

My interviews finally came to an end. Within a few weeks boys began leaving Juja for America, not just lost boys from Sudan but also refugees from Somalia. Every Wednesday a list of names was posted on a bulletin board in the middle of the facility. The moment the list went up, boys crowded around, looking for their names. They shouted and sang when they saw their names. They also called out the names of their new homes in America. The names all sounded very odd, places like Chicago and Atlanta and New York. None of us knew anything about any of the names. We only knew they were in America, and that was enough for us.

A couple of my friends were among the first to find their names on the America list. Within a few days they left Juja for good. Saying good-bye to them was easy. "I will see you in America!" I told them. I watched them climb on the bus for the airport, while I stayed behind, checking the list every Wednesday and wondering what was taking so long.

While I looked over the list week after week, a man named Rob Rogers picked up a bulletin on his way into church near Syracuse, New York. There he saw an announcement that read, "We need host families to serve as foster families for the lost boys from Sudan." He later showed the bulletin to his wife, Barbara, and said, "I think we should do this."

Barbara wasn't so sure. She thought Rob was a little nuts for suggesting it. However, she agreed to attend the informational meeting the following Thursday. Rob had to go out of town on business, which meant Barbara attended the meeting alone. By the time the meeting ended, she was a little nuts herself. She signed the two of them up to become a host family. Over the next few months they attended more classes and had every part of their life investigated by the state of New York. A social worker conducted a home study along with police background checks. Finally a letter arrived telling them that they had been certified by the state to serve as foster parents.

I did not know any of this. All I knew was that my weeks in Juja had turned into months and still my name did not appear on the list.

A worker called me in for my fourth and final interview. This time, the interviewer was not only an American, but an American who had just flown in from the United States itself. He worked for Immigration and Naturalization Services (INS). I knew this interview was very important.

"Are you still in touch with your family back in Sudan?" he asked.

"No. I have not seen or heard from them since I was kidnapped when I was six."

"If you were to find them, would you want to take them to America?"

"They are dead," I said very calmly.

The interviewer paused for a moment. I think my answer took him by surprise. "Okay, then. Uh . . . Why aren't Juja and Kakuma places you can call home?"

"As a Sudanese, I cannot call them home. The rules prevent me from being anything besides a refugee there."

"Why is that not enough for you?"

"I want to do more with my life than survive in a camp." I looked him in the eye. "That is not the kind of life anyone wants."

He did not respond. "What do you want to do in America?"

I broke out in a huge grin. "I want to work hard! I love to work."

The American did not smile back. He looked down at his piece of paper. "Okay. I think that's all I need."

Wednesday rolled around again. Six months had passed since I climbed on the airplane in Kakuma. Most of my friends had left for America. I had begun to wonder if I would ever join them. I walked outside to the bulletin board. A worker had just posted this week's list of names of boys going to America on the next flight. A group of boys crowded around me. A Somali kid tapped the list with his finger and shouted. His friends danced around him. I wished I could be so fortunate.

The board of names was about the size of a large flat-screen television. I scanned down the list from right to left. Once again, my name was missing. However, for some reason, I decided to look one more time. Starting on the left, I read one name after another. All of a sudden, in the middle of the list, I saw it. My heart raced. I could hardly breathe. I had to sit down.

Somalis crowded around the list. I sat off to one side, watching. A couple of them found their names. Their friends kissed them and shouted for joy. "That can't be me," I said to myself. By now I had convinced myself that I had misread the list. Some other boy's name had to be in the middle, not mine.

As soon as the Somalis cleared away, I went back over to the list. I scanned down the middle column. There it was once again, right in the very middle, the words for which I had waited for months. My heart raced again. A smile spread across my face that was so wide my cheeks hurt. I had to sit back down.

A few minutes later I went back to the list. I scanned down the middle column. Those words were still there. I got so excited I could not stand still. I had to sit down. I left for a few minutes, then came back again. And again. And again. Still the words were there, "Joseph Lopepe Lomong, Syracuse, New York." I left a fifth time. When I returned, the *mzungu* who posted the list said to me, "Once you see your name, you can leave. We aren't going to change anything."

"Okay," I said. "Okay. Okay. Okay!" I danced away.

I went back to my dorm and sat on my bunk. "This is it," I said. "It is time to go to America!" I wished I could share my joy with my family in Kakuma. If I had been there when I saw my name on the bulletin board, we would have celebrated. But since they were back in the camp, no celebrations were possible. However, I did not let that get me down.

Joy flowed over me. "When I get to America I will get a job, and then I will really be able to help my friends," I said.

This was my plan.

This was the plan of every boy set free from Kakuma. We went to America not for ourselves, but for every lost boy left behind. I planned to send part of the money I earned back to my friends to help support them and make their lives better. If they could not come to America, I would send as much of America as I could back to them. I knew they would do the same for me. After all, that's what family is all about.

TEN

"Welcome Home, Joseph"

I am a talker. I can talk to anyone, anytime, anywhere. But when I boarded the bus to the Nairobi airport, I had no one to talk to. My friends who traveled to Nairobi with me had already left, and the rest of my family was back in Kakuma. Nearly everyone on the bus came from Somalia and Rwanda. They were funneled through the same refugee processing facility in Juja as the lost boys.

The Somalis and Rwandans laughed and talked in languages I could not understand. All of them wore nice clothes and shoes, much nicer than my one set of Goodwill clothes I brought with me from Kakuma. I felt very out of place in my jeans with the odd pattern. I thought they were stylish when I put them on. After I lived in America a short time, I discovered the only people who wear pants like mine are middle-aged men on a golf course. I had no other clothes and no luggage. All my worldly goods consisted of my airplane ticket and a bag the INS people handed me before we got on the bus. Inside were papers that guaranteed my entrance into the United States. "Hold onto this bag," the officials told us. "Don't drop it or hand it to anyone." I gripped that bag so tight my hand hurt, and I hadn't even arrived at the airport yet.

At the airport, we filed off the bus and into a holding area. The *mzungu* workers in charge handed each of us some bread and a can of Fanta soda. "For me alone?" I asked one of the aid workers. She smiled and motioned for me to take a seat without answering my question. I found a spot on the floor away from the Somalis and Rwandans. I gulped down the soda, but I was not so sure about the bread. I'd never had bread before. I sniffed it and then took a small bite. The bread tasted different than anything I'd had before, but I liked it. However, I could hardly enjoy it because I just knew that at any moment an official would come over and scold me for hogging it for myself. Back in Kakuma, half of a loaf of bread could feed ten people. I felt guilty having so much food all to myself.

The other refugees waiting for our flight did not have the same apprehensions about the food. I watched them take one or two bites, then drop the rest on the floor. I could not believe my eyes. For ten years my friends and I lived on one meal a day. We made every scrap of food last. Yet here in the airport no one seemed to care about how much food they wasted. A couple of the others noticed me staring and yelled something at me. I don't know what they said, but the look on their faces told me they weren't telling me to have a nice day. I moved to the other side of the holding area and waited for more instructions from the *mzungu*.

I did not have to wait long. The *mzungu* made an announcement in English I did not understand. Everyone stood. We lined up again. I shuffled along through the line. Outside through the window I saw the biggest airplane I'd ever seen in my life. The lights flashing on the tips of the wings shimmered on the glass of the airport windows. I'd never seen glass windows before either.

The line moved along until I arrived at the front. An official-looking person examined the I-94 form in my bag. He looked at my photo on the form, then looked at me. He smiled and motioned for me to move forward. I followed the line through a door and outside. Wow! The airplane was huge! An entire village could fit inside it.

"Good luck! Congratulations!" voices called out to me. I turned and saw a huge crowd behind a fence. The fence reminded me of the fence that surrounded the prison camp that my friends and I slipped through late at night when we escaped from the rebels. Everyone beyond the fence smiled and waved at me with so much excitement that I wondered if they were going to America as well. I waved back. Everyone walking in line toward the plane waved. I felt like I was in a victory parade.

The line came to a stairway that went up into the airplane. I looked up at the top. The plane was taller than I had imagined. I walked up to the stairway. Slowly, I lifted one foot and placed it on the first stair. I had one foot in Africa and one foot in America. Joy poured over me. I looked back at the people waving behind the fence. I gave them one final wave, then darted up the stairs. All the suffering of Kakuma, the pain of the civil war in my home country of Sudan, all of it stayed below on the ground. Every step up the ladder filled me with peace.

"Welcome," a beautiful woman at the top of the stairs said in an American accent. "We are so glad to have you onboard."

I smiled. "Thank you," I said in my best English.

She took my ticket. "Follow me," she said. I did as I was told. We walked down one of the two aisles into the main body of the airplane. There were so many seats! The middle section had four seats across, with three on either side of the aisles toward the windows. We walked about halfway back, then she motioned for me to sit in a seat in the middle section next to the aisle.

"Thank you," I said.

"You are welcome. Go ahead and buckle your seat belt," she said.

I shrugged, unsure what to do. The woman reached down, pulled the two belts up, and fastened them for me. She patted me on the leg and said, "Have a nice flight. We are glad you are here."

I smiled in return. The woman left and I settled into my seat. I pulled out a card from the pocket in front of me. It had a diagram of the airplane. That's when I learned this plane was a 747.

The seats on either side of me filled with people. I said hello in Swahili to the Somali woman in the seat next to mine, but she did not understand me. A man's voice came over the PA system and said something in English. I'm not sure what he said. He called himself the captain. That part I got. A few moments later the plane moved backward, stopped, and then moved forward. I leaned forward and tried to look out the window. A few lights passed by, but for the most part, all I could see was dark. The plane moved along the ground, swaying slightly from side to side. The motion and the fact that I could not see out reminded me of the truck that carried me away from my church so many years before. Unlike that long ago trip, everyone around me now wore smiles. No one looked frightened and no one cried. This drive to America was going to be a much better trip!

The drive changed when the plane turned one last time and slowed to a near stop. The engines suddenly grew very loud. We moved forward quickly. The force pinned me back in my seat. The airplane went faster and faster, the engines loud, the sound of the wheels against the ground echoed throughout the cabin. Then, just as suddenly, the front of the plane tilted up, the wheels grew silent, and we were up in the air. I did my best to see out the window. Off in the distance I spied a few lights on the horizon. The plane banked the opposite direction, and the lights disappeared into darkness. That did not matter. I did not need to see anything outside. I felt a great peace because I knew we were on our way to America.

A short time after we took off, the flight attendants wheeled a large cart down the aisles. When they came to me, the attendant pulled out a tray of food and passed it to the woman next to me. She then pulled out another and tried to give it to me. I did not have any money to pay for food. Besides, I had eaten an entire loaf of bread before we boarded the plane. I waved my hand and said, "No, thank you."

"Are you sure?" the attendant asked.

"Yes," I replied. The cart moved on down the aisle. Everyone around me had a small tray of food. It smelled good, but I knew I could wait until we arrived in America to eat. After all, how far away could America be?

A few hours after we took off, the man's voice came over the PA and made another announcement. The plane slowed down. We made a couple of turns and then headed down. Outside the windows I saw lights running up and down streets below us. The plane landed. This had to be America.

"Welcome to Cairo," the captain said. I knew Cairo was not in America. We were still in Africa. When the plane came to a stop, I started to get up. "No, not yet," the flight attendant said to me. I did as I was told. Some people got off the plane, and others got on. Finally, the doors closed, the captain said something over the PA, and we took off again.

Once again, a short time after takeoff, the flight attendants came down the aisle with trays of food. My stomach growled at the sight of food, but still I had no money. When the attendant came to me, I waved my hand again and said, "No, thank you."

The woman next to me said, in English, "Eat." The flight attendant looked at me with a look that told me she really, really wanted me to take the food. But I could not. How would I pay for it? The last thing I wanted to do was land in America with a debt for the food I ate on the way.

Time passed as we flew. I sat in my seat, never once getting up, never once unbuckling my seat belt. My grip stayed tight on the bag the INS people gave me. They told me to hold onto it, and that's exactly what I did. Outside the window, night turned into day then back into night. The trip to America took longer than I ever expected.

Finally we landed. "At last," I said to myself, "America."

"Welcome to Beijing, China," the captain said. I knew we were still not in America. When the plane came to a stop, I stayed in my seat. I had no reason to get off the airplane in China. Some people got off the plane, while others got on. Once everyone found their seats, we backed up from the gate and took off once again.

And once again, not long after we took off, the flight attendants wheeled the cart of food down the aisle. "No, thank you," I said just as I had every other time the attendants offered food to me. By now, I was very hungry. Yet I still had no money. Without money, you cannot eat. Everyone knows that.

The flight attendant looked very concerned when I refused her offer of food. She left the cart and went back to her station in the middle of the plane. While she was gone, the Somali woman handed me a roll from her tray. I was too hungry to refuse it. I gulped it down.

About the time I finished the roll, the flight attendant returned. "Please, take the food," she said.

"I have no money," I said in my best English.

The attendant smiled at me. "Free," she said.

"Free?" That was one English word I knew. "Okay," I said.

She placed the tray in front of me. I did not recognize all of the food, but by this point, I was too hungry for that to matter. I ate the chicken and sauce in the main tray, along with the potatoes alongside it. Next to the bread was a small item wrapped in foil that I had never seen before. I unwrapped it and ate it in one bite. No sooner had I popped it in my mouth than the Somali woman showed me how it was supposed to go on the bread. "Butter," she said. I shrugged and kept eating. The only thing on the tray I did not eat was the green leafy stuff. I tried it, but it did not taste very good.

When I finished my tray of food, the flight attendant brought me another. "Okay," I said with a smile. I ate it nearly as fast as the first tray. We had been on this airplane a very long time. I had grown very hungry.

Outside the window the night turned into day. Off on the horizon I saw nothing but water. Only later did I discover that we had flown over the North Pole on our way from Beijing to New York. My eyes grew heavy, but I fought sleep. I did not want to sleep through arriving in America.

At long last the captain came over the PA and said the words I had waited to hear, "Soon we will land in New York." The plane slowed and banked a time or two. Off in the distance I could see the tall buildings of the city. It was unlike anything I'd ever seen before.

When the plane finally landed, I felt like I was still flying, I was so excited. This was America, the place about which I'd dreamed for so long.

The airplane came to a stop. I stood up for the first time since we left Nairobi. Not once did I get up to go to the bathroom or anything else. I sat in my seat, clutching the bag I'd been told to hold onto. My legs ached when I finally stood, but I did not mind. This was America, at long last.

All the passengers filed off the plane in a line. The line went down a hallway, down a flight of stairs, and up to a man standing behind a wall of glass. "I need to look in your bag," he said. He wore a uniform and badge. An American flag was sewn onto his sleeve. I opened the bag and held it up to him. He pulled out my I-94 form and stamped it. This form allowed me to immigrate to the United States. "There you go," he said. "Next."

I wasn't sure where to go next. Thankfully, an aid worker came over to help. He looked at my airplane ticket and then led me to another terminal area. All around me Americans walked and talked and laughed and went about life as normal. Most were white, but not everyone. This was the first time I realized that all Americans are not white. I assumed they were. Like I said earlier, I thought the cold weather in the United States turned everyone white.

The other immigrants and refugees on the plane went their separate directions. I was the only one in the gate waiting area for the flight to Syracuse. I found a seat, my bag still tight in my hand, and sat down. I do not remember anything else until a man who worked for the airline shook me awake. "We cannot leave without you," he said. Apparently, the moment I sat down I passed out asleep.

The plane to Syracuse was much smaller than the one from Kenya. Thankfully, this time I knew how to use my seat belt. Unlike the first flight, I was the only African on the flight, the only person coming to

America for the first time. Behind me two girls talked and laughed while watching a movie on a portable DVD player. For some reason, their laughter made me feel even better about where I was going.

Thankfully, the flight from New York did not go to Syracuse by way of China. No sooner had we taken off than it felt like we were going back down again. I sat by myself, taking it all in. Outside the window the ground below was very, very green, greener than anything I'd ever seen before. No one offered me any food, although I did get a small cup of soda to drink.

The plane finally landed. Once we stopped, everyone stood up. A line of people filed off the plane. I wasn't sure where to go or what to do, so I followed the line. We walked off the plane and onto a small hallway. Later I learned this hallway is called a Jetway. The hallway led to a door. I walked through and into the airport gate area. I paused for a moment, looking for one of the workers like those who helped me in New York.

That's when I saw it. Right in front of the gate area were a white man and woman. Both wore huge grins. The woman held up a sign with words of English I could understand. There were only three words on it, but they were the best words I'd ever read: "Welcome Home, Joseph."

Ten years after the rebel soldiers ripped me out of my mother's arms, I finally had a place to call home.

ELEVEN

The Promised Land

My new family greeted me with hugs and kisses at the airport. I'd never been hugged or kissed by white people before. They introduced themselves as Rob and Barbara Rogers, "But you can call us Mom and Dad," they said.

"Okay," I said. Mom and Dad were easy to remember. I hadn't called anyone that in a very long time. The words felt good rolling off my tongue.

An official-looking man stood next to them. He reached for the bag I'd held onto since I boarded the bus bound for the airport more than thirty hours earlier. I resisted. "It's okay. I work for the government," he said. Mom and Dad smiled and nodded for me to give him the bag. I did as I was told. The official looked through my bag and then said, "Everything looks good. Welcome to America." He walked away with my bag.

"Do you have any luggage?" Dad asked.

"Yes," I replied. I had no idea what luggage was, but I said yes anyway. *Yes* was the one word I knew I could use and never sound impolite. The last thing I wanted to do was offend these people.

"All right, let's go down to baggage claim," Dad said. Mom took my hand as we started walking. My legs felt shaky and my head was in a fog. Outside the sun shone bright, but my body told me it was the middle of the night. Mom asked me several questions, but I had no idea what she was saying. I knew a little English. Before I left Kenya, I thought I knew a *lot* of English, but speaking words and phrases in a classroom setting is very different than having complex sentences fly at you in an accent you can hardly understand.

We stood at the luggage carousel watching one suitcase after another spin by. "Tell me which one is yours," Dad said. I nodded. I did not understand why we stood there watching suitcases roll by. After most of the luggage had been carried away by other people, Dad came over and looked at my ticket. He gave Mom a look and then said, "I'll go get the car."

Mom led me outside. The air felt so warm and smelled so good. I'd breathed recycled airplane air for far too long. Dad pulled up in the most amazing car I'd ever seen. Only army trucks and jeeps ever came into Kakuma, but this car was nothing like either of them. The green paint shimmered. It was so sleek, so new, I felt like a king climbing inside.

We took off down the road. Everywhere I looked I saw green trees, green grass, and beautiful blue sky. I rolled down the window and stuck my head outside like a dog. I can only imagine what Mom and Dad thought of me in that moment. I didn't know my actions were out of the ordinary. I wanted to smell the sweet, fresh air and take in all the sights rushing past me. What better way to do that than to put my head out the window?

"Joseph, are you hungry?" Dad asked.

"Yes," I said even though my stomach did not feel much like eating.

We pulled into a restaurant and walked inside. The smell of so many different foods nearly gave me a headache. We walked up to the counter. Up above were photos of everything on the menu. I had no idea what was what. So much food from which to choose! All the choices made my head swim. I just knew this had to be one of the nicest restaurants in all of America. Only later did I discover the truth about McDonald's.

My dad ordered a chicken sandwich for me. "For all of us, right?" I asked.

"No. Just for you," he said.

I unwrapped the sandwich, but I could hardly bring myself to eat it. For one thing, my stomach felt queasy from bouncing around on an airplane for a day and a half. But, more than that, I looked at this large piece of chicken sitting on the bread and thought of the way the ten boys in my tent shared one chicken at Christmas and Easter. It did not seem right that I had so much when they had to get by on so little. I took a few bites and wrapped up the rest for later. "We have food at home," Dad said. "You can throw away whatever you don't want." I could not do that. I took the sandwich to the car with me.

Once we were on our way again, Mom turned and said, "We have a surprise for you. Dad found some of your friends here in Syracuse. Would you like to speak to one of them on the phone?"

"Yes," I said.

She handed me a cell phone. It was my first time to talk on the phone. My friend Simon from Kakuma was on the other end of the line. Oh, it felt so good to hear Swahili! Simon left Kakuma a few months before me. He told me how Dad found him and some other lost boys walking down a street in downtown Syracuse. "He asked us about you," Simon said with a laugh, "and we told him you will eat anything and that you talk a *lot!*" Mom and Dad would not discover this was true for a while yet. I loved to talk, but not yet in English.

The car ride home took us down the smoothest four-lane road I'd ever seen. We then turned onto a smaller road, which led to a still smaller one. We topped a big hill, and I could see a lake up ahead. Boats and Jet Skis covered the water. The water was the bluest blue I could imagine. I was trying to take it all in when Dad pulled the car into a driveway and announced, "We're home."

Home? No, someone had to have made a mistake. There is no way I was supposed to end up in a place like this, a place so big and so nice. For starters, there were three other vehicles in the driveway in addition to the car we just came in. The house itself stretched back and forth for a very long distance—at least it seemed like a long distance to me. In Sudan, all houses were small and round. Mom and Dad's house was long and tall. I was amazed. Beyond the house I saw a pavilion and beyond that a pier going out into the water.

"Come on, Joseph. Let's show you around," Dad said.

"Sure, okay," I muttered. I just knew that at any moment an official would arrive, order me into his truck, and take me to where I was really supposed to be, someplace like the dormitory where I stayed in Nairobi.

"This is the garage," Dad said, throwing open a large overhead door. Wow, so much equipment, so many mechanical things. I didn't know what most of them were. However, I did recognize the four bicycles standing on one side. Dad noticed and led me over to them. "This one is mine," he said, pointing. "And that one is our son, Rob's. That one over there is Mom's. And this one," he said as he patted the seat of a brand-new bike, "this one is yours."

"Mine?"

"Sure, if you want it. We have some things out back I think you might be interested in."

After giving me a bicycle, I could not imagine what else Mom and Dad could possibly show me. In Kenya, only the richest people have bicycles. I saw them riding them outside the camp while running my lap around Kakuma. Never in my wildest dreams did I ever expect to have one of my own. It was mine "if I wanted it," Dad said. Who wouldn't want something so wonderful?

I followed Mom and Dad to the back of the house. Dad opened a shed door, revealing a sight like no other. In the camp, we played soccer every day with a ball made of rags. We used to joke about what it would be like to play with a real inflatable ball. Aid workers brought us real balls from time to time, but they did not last long in the heat of the camp. Or maybe they did not last because we played soccer all day every day. And now, inside the doors of the shed in the back of Mom and Dad's house, were enough soccer balls for a year in Kakuma. "We heard you liked to play soccer. Hope these work out for you," Dad said.

My jaw dropped to the ground. In the Bible, the children of Israel dreamed of a promised land that flowed with milk and honey. I found myself in a promised land that flowed with bicycles and soccer balls. *How did I get here?* I wondered. Thirty-six hours earlier I was a poor kid, a lost boy of Sudan with one pair of pants, one shirt, and one pair of shoes. Now I found myself surrounded by riches unlike anything I ever dared dream about.

"Not sure if you play basketball, but we have a few balls for you if you want to pick it up," Dad said. Then he pointed to the fishing poles and the Jet Ski and the other sporting equipment in the shed. He said something about teaching me to use these things, but I did not understand what he said. My mind was too fixated on the multiple soccer balls sitting there, waiting for me to use them. All this was too good to be true. I knew I did not belong in this place. The only question was, how long would it take for these nice people to figure out a mistake had been made and send me on my way?

"Would you like to see the house?" Mom asked. The question blew me away. This shed, this small barn, was bigger than the houses I knew in Kakuma. I thought I would spread my sleeping mat in the barn and live there. There was more to see? My mind could not take it all in.

We walked across the greenest grass I'd ever seen to the back door of the house. "Excuse the mess," Mom said. "This is the laundry room." Back in Kakuma our laundry room consisted of a five-gallon bucket. In America, laundry rooms have large machines that do the wash, but so much more. Stacked on shelves on either side of the room were packages of food and bottles of Coca-Cola. I thought I was dreaming. I'd had my first soda some thirty hours earlier in the Nairobi airport, and I liked it.

I liked it a lot. Apparently Mom and Dad liked it as well. What did I ever do to deserve to be in such a place?

Mom and Dad kept walking, so I did my best to keep up. "This is the kitchen," Mom said. "The fridge is over there and the pantry over there." The next room they called the grandma room, which was the spare bedroom. "And this is the living room," she said. The television in that room caught my eye. The wires behind it did not connect to a car battery. The screen was much larger than the little black-and-white set on which I watched Michael Johnson run.

"Let's head upstairs to your room. You have to be tired after such a long trip," Mom said.

"My room?" I said.

"Of course," Mom said. "Where did you think you would sleep?"

I didn't dare answer. Mom and Dad should have known the answer. They were so nice, but apparently so clueless. Why would they ever think a lost boy like me belonged in their home? I decided to enjoy this place while I could until everyone came to their senses and set things right.

We walked up a set of stairs, then down a hallway. "This is Rob's room," Mom said, pointing toward a doorway on my right. "Our room is just down the hall. And this," she said, pointing into a room that was roughly the same size as the tent where I'd lived with ten other boys for the past ten years, "is your room."

"For me?"

"Yes," she said.

I followed Mom and Dad into the room. Outside, the sky grew dark. "Your bathroom is right through this door," Dad said. "You know how to use a flush toilet, right?"

"Yes," I said. They had not yet figured out that I said yes to everything. The fact was I had never seen a bathroom inside a house. In Africa, you never, ever do your business inside someone's home, especially not in a home this nice. You go to the toilet away from the house so that you do not defile it.

"There's a shower in here as well. And towels in the cabinet there," Dad said.

"Can you think of anything you may need?" Mom said.

"No. Thank you," I said.

"All right, Joseph. We'll let you get some rest. If you need us, we're right down the hall," Dad said.

"Okay," I said.

They left the room and I collapsed on the bed. My brain hurt from all I'd seen and heard since I stepped off the airplane. I'd heard that America was a promised land of plenty, but never this much plenty. I knew there had to be people with so much in the United States, but I never dreamed they might let me stay with them, even if it were for just a night or two. Even the bed was like a fairy tale. All my life I'd slept on a plastic mat that did nothing to cushion my body. The UN handed them out to us to protect us from scorpions in the night. This bed was so soft that I found it difficult to get comfortable. I thought about moving to the floor, but I did not want to upset the Rogers. They told me this bed was for me, so that's where I had to stay. I did not plan on breaking the rules my first night in America.

I lay on the soft bed, my head spinning. My body screamed for sleep and I wanted to give in. However, the light overhead hurt my eyes. I did not know how to turn it off. Apparently in America people slept with light shining in their eyes.

I kicked off my shoes, then crawled under the covers. I pulled the blanket up over my eyes. America was more than I ever dreamed it could be, and I had only been here a few hours. I wondered what the coming days might bring.

TWELVE

A Child Again

I woke up early my first morning in America, confused. I did not yet know the term *jet lag*, but I had a major case of it. I also felt more than a little guilty. My room was so big and so nice, I thought it wrong that I should have so much space all to myself. "I wish my friends in Kakuma could join me here," I said over and over.

Once I heard Mom and Dad stirring about the house, I got up. My appetite had returned. Thankfully Mom had food waiting for me. Unlike Kakuma, meals came more than once a day in the Rogers' home. After breakfast, I wanted to do something I had been unable to do over the past six months in Nairobi. "Dad," I said, "I would like run, then play football, er, soccer."

"Okay, Joseph. You can do that. How far would you like to run?" Dad said.

"Thirty kilometers."

Dad looked over at Mom with a very puzzled expression. "Well, uh, I'm not too good at the metric system, but we can probably arrange that."

"Don't look at me," Mom said. "I have no idea how far thirty kilometers are. You should give Jim Paccia a call. He will know." Jim was the coach of the high school cross-country team.

Dad pulled out his cell phone and left the room. He returned a few moments later with a very shocked look on his face. "You're sure you want to run *thirty* kilometers, not thirteen?" he asked me.

"Thirty, yes," I said.

Dad's jaw dropped. He turned to Mom and said, "That's eighteen *miles*."

Mom's eyes got very big. I did not understand what the big deal was. Every boy in the camp who played soccer ran thirty kilometers before he was allowed on the field. My request seemed perfectly normal to me.

"Well, Joseph, the best I can do is to have you run down the road in front of the house. Follow it down and around until it comes to a big wall called a dam. There and back is fourteen miles. Not quite thirty kilometers, but it's close." Then he turned to Mom and said, "Jim is on his way over."

"Thank you," I said. I started to go out the door. Dad stopped me.

"Hold on. You can't go running down the street barefoot," he said.

I wasn't sure why he said this. I'd run barefoot every day of my life. He walked over to a closet and pulled out a pair of cheap running shoes. "Here, these should fit you."

The shoes fit, but they felt strange to my feet. However, I did not complain or try to take them off. Dad told me to wear these shoes, and so I wore them. Kakuma taught me to follow the rules.

I shot out the door and took off running down the road. The shoes made my feet feel heavy and out of control. I had no connection between the soles of my feet and the earth below me. *These stupid shoes are in the way.* Even with the shoes, I felt the heat of the blacktop. As much as I hated running this way, I knew my bare feet would burn on the asphalt.

Even with shoes, it felt good to run again. The air rushing into my lungs seemed heavier, more humid than what I'd lived with in Kenya. At the same time, I discovered I could run harder without losing my breath. Only later did I learn that I'd spent my entire life in high elevations. Syracuse sits at only 380 feet. I felt like I could run forever here and never grow tired.

The road to the dam took me past beautiful houses with manicured green lawns. Trees towered over the road. I'd never seen trees so tall. Acacia trees have short trunks and large canopies. These New York trees were both tall and broad! Under the trees, white people worked in flower beds and mowed their yards. Dogs barked as I ran by, which made me pick up my pace. In Africa, dogs are not friendly little pets. People use them for protection. Others run wild in packs. Everyone I know has scars from getting too close to a barking dog.

Before I knew it, I reached the dam and turned back toward home. The run back took me up a hill, but I did not mind. Running set me free from all my worries and cares. I did not think about how someone had made a mistake in placing me in this home and how they would show up soon to take me away. Instead I lost myself in the feel of my feet against the smooth pavement and the flow of air rushing past my body.

A little more than a kilometer and a half from Mom and Dad's house, a man stood waiting for me. I knew he was waiting for me, because when I ran past, he started running with me. "Hi, Joseph, I am Jim Paccia, and I'm a friend of your mom and dad."

"Hi," I said, not breaking stride.

The man began breathing hard. He seemed to have a little trouble speaking. "Wow, you sure are running fast," he said between breaths.

I did not understand what he said. I thought he told me I was running too slow. Running slow is one thing I do not do. My parents named me Lopepe, "fast," for a reason. The moment I heard I was running too slow, I thought, *I will show you*, and kicked it into another gear.

The man disappeared in the distance behind me. I ran into the yard and went straight to the shed for the soccer ball. Mom came outside holding a bottle of Coca-Cola. "Would you like one?" she asked.

I nodded with a smile. I love soda.

The man came stumbling up to the house a little while later. I didn't pay much attention to him. Instead I ran around the yard kicking the ball, practicing the moves I'd learned in very heated games in Kakuma. I'd heard they had real soccer teams in America, and I really wanted to join one. We played some games as a team in Kakuma. Our section of the camp went against teams from other sections. That is, those of us from equatorial South Sudan went up against teams of refugees from other parts of Sudan or Somalia or Rwanda. However, we didn't look like a team because we didn't have uniforms. American teams always had uniforms. I'd heard they even had their names on the back. To me, that was the ultimate. If you had your name on the back of a uniform, you had arrived.

I ran again the next day. And the next and the next. Running was about the only thing familiar for me in America. I had to learn everything else from scratch. In some ways, I was like a toddler because I knew nothing about the most basic elements of life here. My first lesson came on my second day in the Rogers' home. Dad came into my room carrying a lamp. "I picked this up for you," he said. "It will be a little more comfortable for you to sleep with this on instead of the overhead light." He plugged in the lamp and set it on a table. After turning on the lamp, he walked over and flipped the light switch down, turning off the overhead light.

So that's how you turn that thing off! Whew. I don't think I could sleep with that thing shining in my eyes another night! That's what I wanted to say, but I didn't know how to say it in English. Instead I simply said, "Thank you." I never slept again with the light, or the lamp, on.

The shower took more time to master than the light. Mom and Dad showed me the shower my first day. "You turn the water on like this," Dad said, lifting up the single handle. Okay, I could remember that. Raise the lever and water comes pouring down from above. It beat bathing with a bucket of water. However, I quickly discovered the shower was not as great as I first thought. The first time I tried to use it, I raised the lever and climbed inside. Brr! That was the coldest water I'd felt in my life. I jumped around, trying to wash and stay warm at the same time, without much success with either. No wonder these people were so white. Showering every day in such cold water had to turn them that way.

I turned the water off and stood there, shivering, waiting for the water to dry. Mom showed me the towels and told me to use one to dry myself, but the towel felt more like a blanket. I couldn't use something so nice to wipe water off my body.

After a few days of frigid showers, I decided to go back to what I knew. I found a large pot in the kitchen and filled it with hot water.

Dad walked in. "What are you doing, Lopez?" By this time I told him my friends all called me Lopez.

"Getting water for shower."

"We have hot water upstairs too," he said.

I gave him a look that told him I thought he was crazy. I caught myself before any words came out of my mouth that might make him angry. "No problem," I said, "I can use this."

"Come on, I'll show you," he said. He led me upstairs and showed me how to turn the lever in the shower and change the temperature of the water. Thank God! I knew I could not take one more cold shower.

"Thank you, Dad," I said. I returned the pot to the kitchen and went back upstairs for a shower. I moved the lever as far from the frigid water as I could and stepped inside. Whoa! I thought the hot water might boil my skin right off of me. I danced around, trying to bathe while avoiding burning myself, without much success with either.

Over the next several days I experimented with the lever, moving it back and forth to several places on the dial. Some days I froze and other days I fried. Finally, after ten or twelve days, I happened to find a place where the water was not too hot and not too cold. From that day until the day I moved off to college, I never moved that lever again!

I learned to use the toilet a little quicker, but it took me a very long time to become comfortable with it. In Africa, you do not do your business inside a house, especially not in a house as nice as Mom and Dad's. For the first few days I could hardly bring myself to use the toilet. Unfortunately, Mom kept offering me Cokes and I kept drinking them. I wanted to go out in the yard, but Rascal, the family dog, was the only one with permission to do his business outside. That left me no choice but to come to terms with an indoor toilet that sat in a room close enough to all the other people in the house to hear what was going on in there.

At first the size and shape of the toilet, to say nothing of the flush mechanism, threw me for a loop. All the toilets I had ever seen consisted of a hole in the ground with a board placed over the top to keep you from falling inside. Needless to say, the indoor bathroom was much nicer than a hole in the ground.

Slowly I learned my way around the house. However, I kept waiting for the day when the Rogers would discover a mistake had been made and I would be forced to leave and go to work. That day never arrived, and I did not understand why.

Instead of forcing me out, Mom and Dad worked to make me feel welcome. They invited the neighborhood teenage boys to come to our house nearly every day. Communicating with these boys was a bit of a problem, but we found a way around it. On warm, sunny days we played soccer in the backyard along with basketball on the driveway. When it rained, which seemed very odd to me that rain could come in the middle of summer, we went inside and played Uno and Mancala. Mancala is actually an African game that my friends and I in Kakuma played using rocks and holes in the ground. I never imagined finding it in America. My new friends also introduced me to a new game with a Swahili name that means "build": Jenga.

I spent a lot of time that first summer playing games with my new friends. Along the way they taught me words in English I had never heard before. Mom quickly pointed out that these were words I should not use, ever.

About a week after I arrived, Mom announced, "Joseph, we need to get you some new clothes." The agency that arranged my stay with them did not tell her or Dad my story. They assumed I would bring clothes with me. I didn't. The first few days I wore Robby's hand-me-downs. Now it was time for clothes of my own.

Mom took me to a large clothing store. When we walked in, I could not believe my eyes. I had never seen so much merchandise in one place. She held up a pair of pants and asked, "Do you like these?"

"Yes," I said. Yes remained my default answer to all questions.

She led me down a few more aisles. "How about this pair? Do you like them?"

"Yes."

"How about this shirt?"

"Yes."

"What about this one?" she said, holding up the ugliest shirt I had ever seen in my life.

"Yes."

"Uh-huh." She put all the clothes down. "Joseph, you do not have to say yes to everything. I need you to tell me what you really think. It will be okay. You won't get in trouble for telling me no."

"Okay," I said.

"So, what about this pair of pants? Do you like them?" she asked.

"Yes," my words said, but my face said no.

"No you don't." She put them down and found another pair I liked much better. "What about these?"

"Yes!" I said. My words and my face finally said the same thing.

"That's better," she said.

She bought several pairs of pants for me, along with shirts, underwear, socks, and a pair of shoes. These were the first new clothes I had ever owned. Everything else I had ever worn came out of the Goodwill box in the camp or had been handed down to me from my older brother. I wondered how I would ever repay her, but Mom waved off my concerns. "I'm your mom," she said. "This is what moms do." I accepted what she said, but I did not fully believe it. Again, I decided to enjoy this moment while it lasted. Once the Rogers came to their senses and sent me off to where I belonged, perhaps they would let me take these clothes with me.

Around my second week in the Rogers' home, Dad told me, "I have a surprise for you today. How would you like to go hang out with your friend Simon and some of the other guys from Sudan?"

"Yes," I said, and this time I meant it. A short time later I found myself in downtown Syracuse, surrounded by old friends. Even though none of these boys had been in my tent, we all knew one another in Kakuma. Seven thousand miles later I felt very close to these boys. These guys were all in their twenties, all except one. That made them too old to be placed with a family, which is why they lived on their own. We spent the afternoon laughing, playing games, and best of all, talking in Swahili. I had not realized how much my ears ached to hear my own language. We talked about old times, and they shared rumors they'd heard about which boys would get to come to America next. It was a great afternoon. I hated to tell them good-bye when Dad came and picked me up.

"Did you have a good time?" Dad asked on the drive home.

"Yes. Very good. Thank you," I said.

"My pleasure," he said. "I'll try to set something up for next week, if you would like."

"Yes; very much."

I did not say much more on the ride home. My poor English made long conversations difficult. That gave me time to think. It felt so good to reconnect with friends from Kakuma. All of us were so blessed to be here.

Then it hit me.

I thought about my life with the Rogers and compared it to my friends in downtown Syracuse. All of us had been robbed of our child-hoods. Most of the boys in Kakuma had to flee their homes or were taken from them prior to their tenth birthdays. I was only six when I was taken. Yet here I was ten years later with an opportunity no other lost boy had, at least no other lost boy that I knew. All of us were lost boys, but thanks to Rob and Barbara Rogers, I got to be a boy in the truest sense of the word once again. My stolen childhood had been returned to me. I did not know how long this could last, but I knew God had given me a priceless gift.

I broke out in a big grin while fighting back tears.

Dad noticed. "Everything all right over there?"

"Yes," I said. "Everything is wonderful."

THIRTEEN

Two Dreams, One Goal

Two people changed the direction of my life forever, and both did it within the first week of my coming to America. The first one changed my life on my second full day here. The man who tried to run alongside me on my fourteen-mile run showed up the next day with a package under his arm. I didn't know who he was, but Mom and Dad did. "Joseph, my name is Jim Paccia," he said, "Coach Jim Paccia."

He had my attention. In Africa, "Coach" is a title of great honor.

"I am very happy to meet you," I said.

"I coach the cross-country team at Tully High School."

I looked at him with a blank expression. He might as well have told me he coached curling or ice dancing. I had no idea what a cross-country team was.

"That's a running team," Dad added. "The cross-country team runs five-kilometer footraces against teams from other schools."

"I am a soccer player," I said. Even after watching Michael Johnson in the 2000 Olympics, soccer was the only real sport I knew anything about.

"Joseph," Coach Paccia said, "after what I saw yesterday, you need to be on the cross-country team. You have a real gift. It would be a shame to waste it."

"I'm a good soccer player," I said.

"I don't doubt that," Coach said. "I think you're probably one of those guys who will excel at any sport they try. But very few people can run like you do. I would love to have you on my team."

I hated to disappoint anyone. "Perhaps one race for you," I said.

"I had something more in mind," Coach said. He reached into his bag. "Joseph, I had this made for you. It's yours if you come out for the cross-country team." Coach Paccia held up a Tully High School team jersey and jacket. The white letters popped off of the all-black background. I was very impressed. Then he turned the jacket around, and my jaw dropped. There, across the back, were the letters L-O-M-O-N-G! For a boy who grew up wearing hand-me-down clothes courtesy of Goodwill, this was the most beautiful piece of clothing I could imagine. A huge grin broke out across my face, but my soccer dreams refused to go down without a fight.

"I can wear this for one race?" I said.

Coach shook his head. "No, not for one race. You only get the jacket if you commit to run the entire season."

This was a hard decision. For ten years soccer had been more than a game to me. Back in the camp, it was a way of life. Running had never been more than a means to an end. If the older boys in Kakuma had never made the rule that we had to run thirty kilometers before we could step foot on the soccer field, I might never have run farther than from one end of the soccer field to the other. In fact, I never even thought of running as a sport, except, of course, for that Michael Johnson guy running for the USA on television.

"Two races?" I said.

Coach Paccia was firm. "No, the entire season. I tell you what I will do. You run this season, you get this jacket. If you run again next season, I'll give you another, and another for the season after that."

I looked at that jacket dangling in front of me. How could I turn my back on something so beautiful? In my mind I saw myself hanging *three* of them in my closet at the end of high school. "Okay," I said. "I will run cross-country."

Less than two months later I ran my first race. Mom and Dad were right there, cheering for me. I was surprised. The sight of them convinced me that I had to win this race, not for myself, but for them. After all, I did not belong here. But now, with this race, I could show them I belonged. In my eyes, this was my chance to show my value and prove that I might be worthy to be a part of a family. This race was my chance to validate my place in America.

However, I had one little problem. Although my English had improved somewhat, I did not fully grasp all the nuances of high school cross-country. In this particular race, a golf cart led the runners around the course. Everyone seemed to understand this little detail except me. I thought I was supposed to beat the golf cart to the finish line.

The moment the gun sounded, I took off after that cart like my life depended on it. Within a few hundred meters I zipped right by it. Once I passed it I did not think it could catch me. I was right. However, the golf cart driver cheated. He took a shortcut and pulled around back in front of me. That just made me run even harder. I passed the cart a second time. He cheated again and got in front of me. Over the course of the first four kilometers of the race, I passed the golf cart several times. I passed him so often that I ran completely out of gas by the end of the race. My huge lead over the cart and the field disappeared. Two guys passed me before I stumbled over the finish line.

Coach Paccia ran over to me. I was fuming. I should have won the race with ease, and I would have if the golf cart had not taken so many shortcuts. Coach grabbed me and said, "Lopez, you ran a great race, but you don't have to run against the cart. You only race the other runners."

Great, I thought. *Now you tell me.*

"I tell you what. In the next race I want you to run alongside the race leaders. Stay right at the front. Then, if you feel up to it, you can run as hard as you want the last mile."

I shook my head to show that I understood. I could hardly breathe, much less talk. Racing a golf cart takes a lot out of you.

A week later we had our second meet. I did exactly what my coach told me to do. When the gun sounded, I took off, but I did not break from the lead pack. Instead I paced myself with the leaders. I enjoyed jogging along with them so much that I tried talking to them throughout the entire race. "Hey, guys, my name is Lopez . . . How long have you been running? . . . Do you play soccer?" I talked and talked and talked even though my English vocabulary was limited. That's just me; I am a talker. However, the other runners did not answer, at least not after the first kilometer or so. The more I tried talking to them, the more they looked at me like I was nuts.

I ran along, talking away until I saw my mom and dad standing at the one-mile marker. Coach told me that he would place them there so that I would know when to start running hard. Mom yelled something like, "Yay, Joseph, you can do it!" She made me laugh. Mom and Dad came to every cross-country meet. They were the only parents who did.

"Hey, guys," I said to the other boys at the front of the pack, "there's my mom and dad. I gotta go. See you at the finish line." With that, I stopped jogging and took off running. I won the meet, beating around four hundred runners from across upstate New York. I received a gold medal that I wore all the way home. Mom and Dad made a huge deal over it, and I let them. This was a very special moment for me.

Our next-door neighbors were outside when we pulled up to the house. Tom and Fran were around eighty years old. They always made me feel very welcome in the neighborhood. "What do you have there?" Tom called out to me.

"A gold medal," Dad answered, his voice brimming with pride.

"Come on over here and let me have a look," Tom said. I was more than happy to show it off. Dad and I walked over to their yard. Tom took a close look at the medal. "Wow, that's something," Tom said.

"He beat a field of four hundred," Dad said.

"Four hundred!" Tom said.

"Yep," Dad said.

"You know, I bet you can run in the Olympics someday for the USA," Fran said.

Fran's words took me right back to watching Michael Johnson on the black-and-white television. "Yes," I said. "That is my goal. One day I will run in the Olympics." Until this moment, the Olympics had always been a far-off dream. Fran nailed it down for me. Running for the USA was no longer a dream. It was my goal, and I would give all I had to reach it.

My mother had another goal for me, and she made sure I gave my all to reach it as well. Within days of my arrival, she told me, "You may be behind now with your education, but we will make sure you catch up. You will graduate from high school on time, and you will go on and get a college education." She did not ask my opinion in the matter. Whether I liked the idea or not, I would finish high school and I would go on to graduate from college. No discussion. No debate. This was just the way it was going to be. It wasn't that she was trying to force something upon me. She knew the value of an education. More than that, she saw within me the ability to reach this dream. She believed all I needed was the opportunity; then I could do the rest. And she moved heaven and earth to make sure I got the opportunity to learn.

At the time, Mom's goal seemed impossible. For starters, I spoke almost no English, and I could read even less. To graduate on time I had to start off in the tenth grade. "He's sixteen," Mom told the school administrator when she enrolled me. "He belongs in the tenth grade." Age-wise, she had a point. However, academically, they should have placed me in kindergarten. I struggled to read, "See Jane. See Jane run. Run, Jane, run." I did not know a consonant from a vowel, and the sounds these strange letters made did not match my Swahili patterns of speech. My math skills were not much better. As for science and history, I did not have a clue.

Mom did not see why such minor details should stand in my way. She made hard and fast academic goals for me, and she would accept nothing less than everything I could give. From day one she worked with me on my English. Every morning she wrote a note for me on the dry-erase board on the refrigerator. I had to figure out what it said. She also placed sticky notes with English names written on everything in the house.

At the same time, she pushed the school administrators and counselors just as hard. Tully High School did not have an ESL program when I arrived in the United States in July 2001. They did by the time I started school that fall, thanks to Mom. She pushed and pushed until the school gave in and started the program. Once classes started, she pushed the school even harder. Whenever a problem arose, she insisted the staff meet with her and settle the issue. After a while the counselors grew afraid of her. I never had anyone work so hard for me.

Once school began, I found it hard to keep up. Mom hired a tutor to help me. Even with the help, there were days my brain ached from it all. At first I did my assignments in Swahili, then translated my work into English. One night I stayed up until two in the morning, pecking away at the computer downstairs, trying to complete a class assignment. Mom never let me get down on myself. "You are very smart, Joseph," she told me over and over. "You can do this. Once your English improves, nothing will be able to stop you."

I believed her. And I kept trying. Thankfully, every school day ended with cross-country practice. Once again, running became my release, my therapy. I did not have to know the difference between a noun and a verb to run as fast as I could. Before long, running became more than therapy. The team became my closest friends.

One of the hardest tasks I faced each day was working the combination on my school locker. Spinning the knob right, then left, then right again made absolutely no sense to me. I could not figure it out. By the time I did manage to open my locker, if I opened it at all, I wasted so much time that I walked in late for my next class. I hated being late. Even though time did not matter in Africa, when it came to schoolwork, you never came into class after the teacher. Coming in late showed a complete lack of respect for the teacher's authority.

Tom Carraci, the captain of the cross-country team, saw me struggling and came up with an idea. "Lopez, as soon as class ends, I will meet you at your locker," he said. "I'll open it, and you can grab your books and go." I was never late for class again. Tom and I became best friends, and we still are to this day. Those first few weeks of school, I felt very alone in a foreign place. Tom stepped up and helped me navigate through school life. He taught me the meaning of friendship in America.

My first semester didn't go so well. I failed a few of my classes. Adjusting to the classroom and the constant barrage of English presented enough challenges, and the school environment made life even harder. I had never seen such displays of public affection like I saw in the halls of Tully High School every day. In Africa, boys and girls do not hold hands and kiss. And the teachers struck me as odd, but in a good way. I'd never had a teacher who did not beat me when I made a mistake. Although I preferred not getting swats for messing up a math quiz, it took some getting used to. I guess all the changes were too much. I ended up failing a couple of classes.

Mom didn't care. She marched up to the school and announced that I would be given the opportunity to take my failed classes the following summer. No one argued the point with her. The following summer, I passed every class I had failed before.

Long before passing my classes in the summer, one teacher turned school around for me. My history teacher, Miss Riley, opened my eyes to a larger world I never knew existed and made me love school in the process. She found a way to connect with me and to connect my interests with learning.

During the unit on World War II, everyone had to write an essay on some topic connected to the war. I had no idea what to choose. Up until a few weeks earlier, I had never heard of World War II, or World War I for that matter. Miss Riley noticed I was struggling.

"What are you most interested in, Lopez?" she asked.

The answer was easy. "Running," I said. "I am going to run in the Olympics."

Miss Riley nodded like she knew something I did not. She pulled a book off a shelf and handed it to me. "Have you ever heard of Jesse Owens?" she asked.

I shook my head.

"I think you will like learning about him. Why don't you read this and write your essay about him?"

I looked at the book cover. Jesse Owens was black, like me, and he was a runner! "Okay," I said.

Let me tell you, that book and that class opened up my eyes to see my Olympic goal as far bigger than sports. Jesse Owens competed in the 1936 Olympics, which were held in Nazi Germany. Hitler planned on using the Olympics as a way of showing the superiority of the Aryan race, but Jesse Owens singlehandedly shoved that in his face. Not only was Owens an American, he was black as well, which made Hitler madder still. Jesse Owens refused to back down and, in the process, made a statement to the world.

Jesse Owens inspired me. I made up my mind that I wanted to be like him. Yes, I was going to compete in the Olympics, but I would do more than compete. I would use success as a runner to make a difference in the lives of others. To do that, I needed an education. I made up my mind. I could reach this goal as well. Just like my Olympic dream, all I needed was to work hard and refuse to let failures get me down. If I did that, the rest would take care of itself.

FOURTEEN

9-11

The bus dropped me off at school. I still felt a little out of place here. It was only my third week of school. Trying to communicate with my teachers and fellow students left me frustrated. I felt most comfortable around the guys on the cross-country team. Running is a language all its own, and I spoke it pretty well. Mom and Dad and I understood each other a little better, although no one understood me as well as Rascal, the family dog. He and I were on the same wavelength from the start.

I weaved my way down the halls, past the overly affectionate couples near the front door, and through the group of freshman boys huddled together near the gym. Freshmen stood out because they were so much smaller than everyone else.

The first bell rang. I went to my first class. The teacher lectured. I tried to tune my brain into English. I still thought and dreamed and daydreamed in Swahili. Switching to English was like tuning in a radio station that is just out of range. Forty-five minutes later the bell rang. First period ended.

I headed to my locker. The mood in the hallway felt different. Something odd seemed to be going on, but I had no idea what. With the language and cultural differences, normal days felt odd to me. Even so, something felt even more abnormal than usual between first and second period. I overheard a few people talking about a plane crash, but I did not stop to ask questions. Next period was Miss Riley's history class, and I did not want to be late.

Tom waited at my locker for me. He wore a worried look. "What's going on?" I asked him.

"I'm not sure. A plane crashed in New York. It hit the World Trade Center. I heard it looks pretty bad," he said.

"That's terrible," I said. I didn't know much about plane crashes or New York. I thought it might be far away, but I was not sure. My flight from New York to Syracuse didn't last long, which made me think it had to be close by.

"Yeah," Tom said. "You good here? I gotta get to class."

I grabbed my books. "Yep. Me too. See you at practice."

"See you then," Tom said and took off. I slammed the locker shut and hurried to Miss Riley's class. I got there before the bell rang, which was always my goal. I hated being late for class. When your name is Fast, there is never an excuse for arriving late.

The bell rang. Class started. Miss Riley took roll. "Ann?" "Here." "Carl?" "Here." "Lopez?" "Here." The day was exactly like any other school day. "Turn to page thirty-seven of your textbook," Miss Riley announced. Pages ruffled throughout the room. She started lecturing on some place far away, and I did my best to keep up with her. Even though my language skills had improved since July, I still had trouble following long, fast, complex sentences in that distinctive American accent. I think I caught about two-thirds of her lecture, which was a lot better than the zero percent I would have caught just three months earlier.

Maybe fifteen minutes into Miss Riley's class, the bell rang. Everyone jumped, startled. The bell wasn't supposed to ring for another thirty minutes. It rang again, stopped, then rang again and again and again. I looked around the room. Everyone had the same confused look as me, including Miss Riley. "Fire drill?" I asked someone close by.

"Doesn't sound like a fire drill to me," he said. "Fire drill is one long blast, not this on and off."

The bell rang one last time. Half the class stood up; part of us stayed seated. No one knew what to do.

The principal came over the intercom. "All students proceed as quickly as possible to the auditorium. Leave your books and leave now."

Miss Riley stood. "You heard the announcement. Leave your books and line up at the door." She led us out into the hall, which was now packed with people. A group of girls walked by, all of them crying. I glanced around. Even guys were crying. I heard someone say something about a second plane. A couple of people near me talked about an attack and war. *Why would anyone in America use such words?* Fear filled the hallway. The looks on the faces reminded me of my days long ago of running into caves with my family when the Sudanese jets flew over our village. I had no idea what was going on, but I seemed to be the only one. Everyone else seemed to understand that something horrible had taken place.

We filed into the auditorium and sat down. Televisions had been placed on the stage where everyone could see them. All the talk died down. Everyone stared at the televisions. I recognized New York City on the television screen from when I flew into it back in July. However, New York was nothing like it was the day I flew in, or anything like I'd seen on television since. People on the streets ran in fear. A few stopped and looked up. Most cried hysterically. Up above them all, smoke poured out of the Twin Towers of the World Trade Center. The television announcers explained that the buildings had been attacked by terrorists. I did not know what a terrorist was, but the images on the screen made it clear what they were all about.

I stared at the television in total disbelief. *How could war follow me here?* When I was in Kakuma, America was next to heaven. Everything

I'd experienced since arriving only confirmed this belief. America means peace. Here, you are safe from war. Back in Sudan, war was inescapable. Even though our village was never attacked by government forces, my friends in Kakuma had their villages bombed into extinction. No one in America worried about bombs dropping on their homes, or at least I did not think they did. Watching the scenes from New York, now I was not so sure. I thought I'd left death and destruction behind me. I was wrong.

The school principal kept us in the auditorium for a little over an hour. On the television screen the nightmare grew worse. One of the Twin Towers collapsed on itself. The newspeople said as many as ten thousand people might be in the building. Their numbers were wrong, but no one knew it on this Tuesday in September 2001. About the time the first tower collapsed, the principal walked onstage and said, "Another plane struck the Pentagon. We have decided to dismiss school for the rest of the day. Everyone needs to go straight home. Buses are in front of the school. Go home immediately."

On the way out of the school building, everyone cried. No one in the school had ever lived through war before, not war in their own country. No one except me.

In front of the school, confusion reigned. Cars and vans jammed the drive along with school buses. I looked and looked for my bus. The bus had a rabbit painted on the side, which made it easy for me to find. I did not see it anywhere. I stopped and asked one of the teachers who directed traffic outside which bus I should now take. He pointed to one, and I climbed on. Thankfully, it was the right bus. Onboard the bus, more kids cried. Looks of sheer terror surrounded me. This could not be America.

No one was home when I got off the bus. I called Mom and asked her what I should do. "Stay inside," she said. "Dad and I will be there soon." I turned on the television and watched the news coverage for a little while. The second building collapsed. A chill ran down my spine. I thought back to a conversation a few weeks earlier when Mom and Dad had talked about taking me to New York City. "We will go to the tallest buildings in the world," they said. They meant the World Trade Center. *We could have been there just a month earlier,* I thought.

I sat and watched the television. Smoke and dust covered New York City. I was scared. This looked worse than anything I'd heard about in Sudan. The home phone rang almost nonstop. Another plane crashed, this time in Pennsylvania. The newspeople said the White House might be the next target. I could not keep watching. I turned off the television and went outside to wait for Mom and Dad to come home. Images of people fleeing New York on foot across the bridges felt far too familiar. I had to get away from it.

Mom and Dad arrived a short time later. Both were visibly shaken. I sensed they too were very afraid. Mom hugged me and asked, "Are you okay?"

"Yes," I lied. My new country, my home, had been attacked. I had no idea where New York was. For all I knew, the World Trade Center and the Pentagon could be nearby. Earlier in the day I saw planes flying overhead, which made me wonder if Syracuse might be attacked next.

"Let's go inside," she said.

"Okay," I said. We went inside. Dad turned on the television. I did not want to watch. I'd experienced war. Watching the start of another did not appeal to me. But I did not say anything. Instead I sat on the couch and watched with Mom and Dad.

A newscast showed a scene from the other side of the world. People celebrated. Al-Qaeda claimed responsibility. I recognized that name. They had ties to the people who bombed villages in South Sudan. I felt like I was back there again. Every time we saw a fighter jet in Kimotong, we ran to a cave for shelter. I didn't know where to run here in Tully. Maybe we didn't have any place to hide. What, then, were we to do when the planes attacked us?

Dad could tell I was afraid. "You know you are safe here, no matter what you see on television," he said.

"Yes, I know," I said.

"We don't know where all of this will lead," Mom added, "but it will never be like it was in Africa. This is an isolated attack. You don't have to worry about an attack around here."

"I understand," I said. I watched them closely. Their actions matched their words. Yes, they were upset over the attacks, but they had a strength about them that told me everything would be okay. We watched the news for a while longer. After a while I announced, "I'm tired. I think I will go to bed."

Mom and Dad both hugged me good night. I went upstairs and climbed into my bed. As bad as this day had been, it was very different from the war back home. Lying there in the dark, listening to the television downstairs, I knew that in spite of everything I'd seen and heard that day, I was safe. However, my illusions about America being a land of peace were shattered. Bad people are everywhere. Unfortunately, that is a part of life no matter where you live.

Over the next few days I discovered how different America was from Sudan. Back home, we had to run and hide. We didn't have a way to stand up and fight. Then I saw President Bush on television, standing in the midst of the carnage in New York, a bullhorn in his hand. Rescue workers stood all around him. I could hardly understand anything he said, but the image of him standing there was the most powerful thing I'd ever seen. He inspired me more than words can describe. Watching him there, I knew I was safe.

The next day I went to school, a table was set up in front selling T-shirts. I picked one up. There across the front were the words "United We Stand" with an American flag in the background. I bought one. Everyone in school bought one. We all wore them the rest of the week. This was another change for me. I realized the American people love their country and, more important, are extremely proud of it. I had never been proud to live in Sudan. I never knew it was possible to be proud of a country. I was proud of our community, and I was especially proud of my mother and father and all their hard work to provide for us kids. I always walked with my back straight and proud when I walked with my father to our farm or helped him with our cattle. But I had never been proud of my country.

Now I was. I would not become a citizen of the United States until 2007, which was the earliest I could become a citizen, but after September 11, I was an American. The terrorists' attacks bonded the country together, and it made me a part of it as well. This new place was now my home, a home I loved and was proud of, a home I hoped to represent someday and make my home proud of me as well.

There was another casualty of the September 11 attacks that very few people knew about at the time. In the wake of the attacks, the United States halted the program that brought me and many other lost boys to America. Heightened concerns over security left officials wary that terrorists might sneak into the country posing as lost boys. I had friends waiting in Kenya whose entry into the United States was delayed indefinitely.

Although a few boys were allowed into the country a few months later, the resettlement program did not begin again in earnest until 2004. By then, it was too late for many of the boys I knew in Kakuma. The screening process became much stricter. Those who were in line to come over here in 2001 who did not get in after 9-11 found they had to start the process all over again. I have friends who were supposed to come to America, but they never did. That could have been me. Knowing this only strengthened my resolve to take full advantage of the opportunity I had received, not only for myself, but for all the lost boys left behind.

FIFTEEN

They're Alive?

I settled into life in upstate New York. My days revolved around school, cross-country practice, and homework. Race days were the best. As part of my pre-race ritual, Dad woke up early in the morning to cook me a special breakfast. He made the usual eggs and toast, but he also had a secret ingredient that he said was the key to running fast. On race days he cooked crispy strips of zebra for me. "This is our secret," Dad told me. "You don't want those other guys to start eating zebra and outrun you, do you?" Of course I did not want that. I loved zebra. Every race day morning, I hurried into the kitchen, sat at the table, and ordered "zebra." Afterward I went out and crushed the other kids. Perhaps I am too trusting, but it took a year and a half before I figured out the secret to my success was really bacon, not zebra.

The weather turned cold early my first fall in Syracuse. At least I thought it was cold. When you grow up in a place that sits just above the equator with an average temperature of 104 degrees twelve months a year, any temperature below eighty feels like an arctic blast. By October the temperature in upstate New York rarely climbs above seventy. I thought I'd moved to the North Pole.

One Saturday we caught a break. The sun came out, the temperature warmed, and it was a perfect fall day. Mom suggested we take advantage of the weather and spend the day on the lake. "We probably won't get another chance like this until next spring," she said. The concept of spring was new to me. Equatorial Africa has two seasons, the dry season and the rainy season. We call the rainy season winter. The dry is summer. Spring and fall do not exist.

Dad got the boat ready, while Mom packed a picnic lunch. I found a heavy jacket to wear. A warm fall day still felt cold to me. We loaded ourselves into the boat and pushed out into the lake. Hills rose up from the water on all sides, with every hill covered by a sea of trees. I thought the trees looked amazing in the summer. Now that fall was here, the explosion of colors took my breath away. I did not know it was possible for leaves to turn red and orange and yellow. I sat and stared out at the show as Dad motored the boat out into the middle of the lake. The warm sun felt good against the cool air rising up from the water.

Dad stopped the boat. Song birds filled the air with music. I could not imagine a more beautiful or peaceful place on the planet.

"Are you hungry, Joseph?" Mom asked. She always calls me Joseph. Dad and all my friends call me Lopez.

This was a silly question. I was *always* hungry even though I ate all the time. Mom loved trying to make up for all the meals I'd missed in Kakuma. It was a good thing I ran several miles every day, or we might have needed a bigger boat to float me out into the lake. "Very hungry," I said.

"Chicken?" she said, holding out the basket.

"Yes," I said. I plunged my hand down into the basket and pulled out a huge piece of chicken. Mom was a great cook. I couldn't get enough of her food.

I sat back and munched on the chicken. Dad took a piece. "You know, this is pretty much a perfect day," he said.

"We never had days like this in Kakuma," I said. "It was always hot and dry. The wind kicked up dust storms that made it hard to breathe. We didn't have any grass, only dirt. I don't know if grass would not grow, or if all the people trampled it down."

"That had to be a hard place to live," Mom said. I could tell she had a lot of questions, but she didn't ask them. This was the first time I had talked about what life was like in the refugee camp. Mom and Dad were very respectful of my past. They never tried to get me to open up about what I'd been through. I didn't want to talk much about it either. The past was the past. I had a new life in America. Besides, I didn't dare say too much about my old life. If Mom and Dad found out the truth about me, they would realize that I did not deserve to live in such a nice place.

However, after four months in the Rogers' home, I realized I was not here by mistake. Mom and Dad wanted me here. A little light clicked on for me during the cross-country season. They came to every single meet. They never missed one. No other parents came to all the meets, or hardly any others did. But mine were always there. And they weren't just there; they cheered for me and celebrated when I won like I was their real son. That's when I started to understand that they genuinely loved and cared about me.

"Very hard," I said. I paused for a moment, took a deep breath, and started talking. I talked for a long time. Mom and Dad sat and listened. I told them how the soldiers stole me from my mother's arms at church in Kimotong and took me to a prison camp. I told them about escaping in the night with my three angels and our three-day run across the savannah. When I came to America, the Rogers knew nothing about me except for the fact that I was one of the lost boys of Sudan. Now it was time to tell them my story, and I held nothing back. I talked about day-to-day life in Kakuma and how we looked forward to Tuesday trash day for our best meal of the week.

I talked and talked. Mom cried. Dad fought back tears. For me, I felt more than relieved to finally have my story out there. I felt at home. That day on the lake, Rob and Barbara Rogers stopped being two very nice but naive *mzungu* who allowed me to live in their house. They became my mom and dad.

Hearing my story affected the two of them as well. They had already figured out I was lonely. I went from living with ten brothers in a very small space, to being an only child in a really big house. Robby, Mom and Dad's biological son, came home from college on holidays and some weekends, but it was not the same. I love Robby and think of him as my brother, but I wanted someone close by all the time. At first I was afraid to say anything to Mom and Dad. However, once I opened up about the rest of my life, I didn't see any point in holding back. "I would like to have another lost boy live here. I have lots of room in my room."

"I think that's a good idea," Dad said. I could not believe my ears.

"Really? Are you serious?"

"Of course I am serious. It will take a while to get approved for another son. That will give us time to get the house ready."

I didn't know what we had to do to get the house ready besides throw another bed into my room. Dad had bigger plans in mind. "We need to add another closet," he told me, "and I want you to help me. What do you think? Are you up to it?"

I had no idea what I was getting myself into when I uttered my favorite English word, "Yes."

Dad's idea of adding a closet meant more than adding a wall or two inside my room. The roof of the house sloped down at my room, which made the ceiling come down at an odd angle on one side. "We're going to open up the roof and add a dormer," Dad explained. "That should give you some head room and make space for another closet."

"What's a dormer?" I asked.

Dad laughed. "Don't worry about it. I just need you to be my gopher."

"A what?"

"When I need something, you grab it. Gopher means you 'go for' things for me."

"Okay," I said. I didn't get the joke.

The weather turned brutally cold the Saturday we started the remodel. I knew absolutely nothing about construction then, and I still know very little about it today. However, within the first five minutes of our remodel, I figured out one little fact: when you cut a hole in the roof and expose the inside of the house to the weather outside, it is best to do it in the summer. We did not do our project in the summer. No, we did ours in the middle of my first winter.

I also learned pretty fast what a go-for is. "Hand me the saw, will you Lopez? . . . I need the hammer . . . Bring up those two-by-fours . . ." I flashed back to Sudan helping my father on his farm. I love to help. However, I never helped on the farm in winter in Sudan since we don't have winter back there. We sure had winter in Tully, New York.

I handed Dad a saw and then waited for my next set of instructions. Before I knew it, I could not feel my fingers in my gloves. My toes felt like they'd already fallen off from the cold. I waited for Dad to ask me to go get something. He looked like he had everything he needed up on the roof. I sneaked inside the house and went straight to the kitchen, where Mom was. "It's c-c-c-cold," I said.

"Oh, Lopez," she said in that Mom tone. "Would you like some hot chocolate?"

"Yes, very much."

I sucked down the hot chocolate as fast as I dared. Then, from outside, I heard Dad yell, "Lopez, where did you go? I need you."

I sat my hot chocolate on the counter, pulled my gloves back on, and went back out into the cold to help. Half an hour later, I was back in the kitchen drinking hot chocolate. "Lopez, where did you go?" Dad yelled. I pulled my gloves on and went back out to the cold. He and I did this dance for the next couple of weekends until the room was finished.

One evening after a day of working on the remodel, Dad and I warmed up in the hot tub. For no particular reason, he looked at me and asked, "When you first got here, why did you say yes to everything?

When you needed something or didn't know something, why didn't you just ask? Why did you say yes and go along to get along?"

"Honestly?" I asked.

"Yes, honestly, why did you do it?"

I was ashamed to answer. Finally I forced the words out. "I was afraid I would make you mad and you would send me away. I knew I was not supposed to be here."

"What are you talking about?"

"I thought someone made a mistake letting me live in this nice place. I thought if I made you mad, you would send me away."

"Why on earth would you think that?"

"Because all this is too nice to be real. I do not deserve it, or people like you and Mom."

Dad looked at me with a mixture of shock and sadness. "Son, you know better than that now, don't you?"

I could hardly look him in the eye. I was ashamed at what I had once thought of him and Mom. "Yes, Dad, I do."

"Listen to me. This is your home. It always will be. Nothing can change that, and nothing can change how we feel about you. Do you understand?"

"Yes, yes, yes," I said.

If I ever had any doubts about where I stood in the family, they disappeared completely when I tried to get a learner's permit to drive. The state of New York had a rule against foster children getting driver's licenses. I do not know why they had this rule. Perhaps they thought the moment we got behind a wheel we would take off for Canada or something. The rule made no sense to me or to my dad. And he tried to do something about it.

Dad took me into Syracuse for a meeting with my case worker and some official in charge of foster care in upstate New York. I did not know who everyone was in the room, but I knew they wielded a great deal of authority. The meeting started with the officials telling my dad why I could not get my driver's permit. Dad cut them off. "You let these boys come into this country, and you tell them that it is now their home, but then you make all these rules that tell them they don't belong here. Well let me tell you, you can either waive this rule and let Lopez get his learner's permit, or I am going to go find a judge who will slap an injunction on you so fast it will make your head spin. So what's it going to be?"

The officials in the room had clearly never been spoken to in such a manner. They stammered around and spouted more of their rules, but my dad would have none of it. He kept pressing and pressing until they gave in. Right then and there, I knew my dad loved me. No one had ever stood up for me before, ever.

A few weeks after we finished the remodel, life got even better at home. Since I first arrived in America, Mom and Dad arranged for me to go hang out with the other lost boys in the area at least once every couple of weeks. All the boys were older and had jobs, all but Dominic. Dominic was my age, but due to a clerical error when he first came to America, he lived with the older lost boys in downtown Syracuse instead of living with a family. It wasn't a good situation for him. All that changed the day after the state of New York approved Mom and Dad to take in another foster son. They chose Dominic. The courts signed off on the decision, and he came to live with us.

When Dominic moved in, I showed him around. I took him to our room, pointed at the remodeled part, and announced, "Dad and I did this together."

"What? The two of you did this?"

"Yes," I said proudly. I didn't see any point in telling him that I spent most of my time running back and forth to the kitchen for hot chocolate.

"Wow," Dominic said. He looked all around the room. "Next year, I want to do a construction project with Dad!" I think he made Dad's day.

A few months later a third brother moved in. Peter came from Kakuma. He was one of the few lost boys allowed to immigrate after 9-11. Once the three of us were together at home, nothing could stand in our way. Now I was the big brother once again. I showed Peter all the things I did not know when I first came to America, like how to turn off the lights and how to adjust the hot and cold water in the shower.

Dominic, Peter, and I were inseparable. Before they came, our family went out to eat every Friday night. Mom and Dad meant it as a treat, but for me it was sheer torture. I had no idea what to order. The photos of food on the menu did not help. But once Dominic and Peter arrived, Friday nights became a blast. One of us would pick out something on the menu, and the other two of us immediately announced, "Yep, we'll have that too!" The three of us also ran together. The first spring Dominic lived with us, before Peter arrived, he and I became a force on our track team. I ran everything Coach Paccia asked me to run: the mile; the 800-meter run, which is two laps around the track; the 4-by-800 relay where I ran the anchor leg; the triple jump and long jump—it did not matter. Dominic was the same way. We did whatever Coach needed to help the team win the meet. In track, you score points for the team based on where you finish in individual races. First place scores ten team points; second place, eight; third, six; fourth, four; and on down the line. Between Dominic and I, we often scored eighty points for the team. Needless to say, other high schools probably wondered where they could get lost boys for their track teams.

Life was good. Very good. But life never stands still, even in the good times.

An early summer day in 2003, I sat in the backyard with Dominic and Peter. The phone rang. Mom answered. "Sure, just a minute," she said. Then she looked at me. "Joseph, Simon wants to talk to you." Simon is the lost boy I called on my way home from the airport the day I arrived. By now we were very good friends. We talked all the time. The fact that he called did not strike me as odd in any way.

I grabbed the phone. "Simon, what are you doing, my friend?" I said in Swahili. We always spoke to one another in Swahili.

"Someone was in Kakuma today looking for you," he said.

"For me?" I asked. "Who could possibly have been looking for me in

Kakuma?" My friends were all either in Kakuma already or had resettled in the United States.

"Your mother."

"What?" My heart jumped into my throat. I started to say that that was impossible because my mother is dead. But I stopped myself. I did not know for certain my mother was dead. That was something I had to tell myself to survive the refugee camp.

"Your mother came to Kakuma looking for you. She heard two of your friends talking about how they wished Lopez had been on the soccer field today. She asked who they were talking about. They said you. She wanted to know where you were, and they told her you are in America. They called me. I have a cell phone number for your mother if you want to call her."

All the time I am talking to Simon, my American mom is watching me. The look on my face told her my world had just flipped upside down. "Okay," I said. I found a piece of paper and wrote down the number. "Thanks," I said and hung up the phone.

"What's going on, Joseph?" Mom asked.

"It's my mother," I said. I could not force myself to say anything more. I could not make up my mind if I believed what I had just heard.

"Your mother? What?" Mom asked.

I looked up at Mom; tears filled my eyes. "My mother is alive. Here's her phone number."

"Call. Call right now," Mom said.

"I don't know if I can," I said.

"I'll dial the number for you," she said. And she did.

The next thing I knew, I heard a voice on the phone I could not even remember. "Lopepe?" she said.

"Yes, this is Lopepe," I replied.

My mother had not heard my voice since I was six years old. I was now eighteen. She expected the voice of a child, not a full-grown man. "No, this does not sound like my Lopepe. You must be the wrong child."

My mother spoke Buya, not Swahili. I had not heard Buya since my three angels disappeared from Kakuma. I could hardly understand what she said.

"Mother, it is me. Lopepe. The soldiers tore me from your arms when I was six years old." My voice cracked. Tears flowed down my face.

"Lopepe . . ." My mother wept on the other side of the world. "Lopepe . . . you're alive," my mother said.

"Yes, Mother, I am alive." I wept. "And Father, is he . . . ?" I could not finish my sentence.

"Yes, he is alive. Where are you?"

"America," I said.

"You are alive?" my mother said over and over.

"Yes, Mother, I am alive."

The two of us tried to say more, and maybe we did. To be honest, I do not remember what we said. The words did not matter. All we needed to hear was the sound of the other's voice. For years I had wondered, and now I knew, they were alive.

My mother and father were alive.

SIXTEEN

"This Place Will Take You to the Olympics"

When are you coming home, Lopepe?" my mother asked. She asked the same question at least ten times during our twice weekly phone calls. The first time she asked, my stomach knotted up on me and a lump jumped into my throat. How do you tell your desperate mother who had returned from the grave that she still may never see you again? By now I had answered the question enough times that I did not feel the rush of emotion.

"Mother," I said, "I explained that to you. I live in America now. I am in school. I am going to go to college and get an education. I cannot come back to Africa now."

"No, no, no, Lopepe. You need to come home."

"That is impossible. America is very far away. I cannot come home."

My mother's concept of distance mirrored my own before I climbed on the 747 bound for New York by way of Beijing. "Will you come home today?" she asked.

We had a variation of this conversation at the end of every phone call. She wanted me back home. I could not blame her. After the rebels took me from my church, my family searched for me, to no avail. Eventually they decided I must be dead. My family buried the few items I'd left behind. The entire village turned out for my funeral. They mourned me for weeks, but they never forgot me. Even after my funeral, my mother never gave up her dream of finding me. Now that she had, I had to come home.

But I could not go back to Africa, not yet at least. My mother wanted me to come back to the only life she had ever known, but my world and my dreams went far beyond taking care of my father's cows. To return to Kimotong now meant giving up my goals of a college degree and running in the Olympics. I must have inherited some of my mother's determination that made her search for her dead son for a dozen years, for I was determined never, ever to give up on my goals until I either reached them or gave my all trying. I knew God gave me these dreams. How could I give up on them?

The thing about dreams, though, is they usually sound crazy to everyone but you. All it takes is one other person to buy into them to keep you going. At the start of our first cross-country practice of my junior year, Coach Paccia sent the entire team running up a hill that overlooked Tully High School. Tom Carraci and I took off in front of the rest of the team. Tom is the same friend who opened my locker for me every day my first year at Tully. Coach Paccia was supposed to run up the hill with us, but his bad knees kept him from keeping up with Tom and me.

Tom and I raced up the hill. I don't remember who won that round. After all, this was just a warm-up for the real practice. We stood on top of the hill, hands on hips, trying to catch our breath. Down below, the lacrosse team practiced on one field, the football team on another. "Did I tell you, Tom, that I am going to run in the Olympics in 2008?"

"Only about a million times," Tom said. "Tell you what: when you make the team, I am going with you to the Olympics. I don't care where it is; I will be there to watch you run."

Another member of the team, one of my best friends named Sean, came up at the same time. "Me too. When you run in the Olympics, I'm going too."

"Really?" I said.

Tom looked at me with complete seriousness. "If anyone can do it, you can. And when you do, I'm going to be there."

This was a big moment for me. I knew I had the ability to make my dream come true, but it is one thing to believe in yourself. It is something else entirely to have friends believe in you as well.

"It's a deal, then," I said. "You're both going with me to Beijing, China, in 2008!"

"You got it," Tom said. He shook my hand to seal the deal, as did Sean. 2008 was five years away. I was a skinny high school junior—well, sort of skinny. Mom fed me so well that I was starting to look more like a football player than a runner. That did not matter. My dream would come true.

My second year of high school in America I won the state cross-country final, which qualified me for the national regional high school championships. I finished twelfth in my region. The next year, my senior year, I did even better. After winning state, I finished in the top six in the national regionals. I then traveled to San Diego for the Foot Locker National High School Championships. I did not win the Foot Locker Championships, but I did well enough for college recruiters to come calling. Big schools recruited me, schools like Oklahoma, Florida, even Princeton. Unfortunately, my SAT scores kept me from qualifying for a Division 1 scholarship right out of high school. I could have gone to a nearby junior college to get my prerequisite classes out of the way. If my grades were good enough, I would have been eligible for a scholarship without my SAT scores.

But going to a junior college near Syracuse, or any other school in upstate New York, was not an option. Dominic and I graduated at the same time, and we both had the same plan for college. Of course, we planned on getting our degrees. Mom made it clear we had to get our degrees, end of discussion. However, the way we saw it, if we can get a college education anywhere, we ought to get it someplace warm. After three years in upstate New York, I'd had my fill of cold weather.

Mom came up with a highly scientific way of finding a college for two former lost boys who wanted to get out of the cold: during spring break, she loaded us in her car and drove south. We did not bother to stop anywhere in New York or Pennsylvania. Mom took us to a handful of colleges in Maryland, but none of them felt right to me. We kept going south.

On our second day of driving, we arrived in Virginia Beach, Virginia. Mom had set up an appointment for us at Norfolk State University. As soon as we drove onto the campus, I thought, *This is the place for me*. The campus tour sealed the deal. The day was warm, the campus green and beautiful, and the school seemed just the right size to me, not too small and not too large. Norfolk State also happened to be a predominantly black school, which appealed to me. I did not want to stand out in this new place.

Mom arranged for us to meet the track coach, but she kept the meeting very low-key. For her, academics and finding a place where we would actually graduate meant more than anything else. If she had mentioned the fact that I was the number one cross-country runner in the state of New York, the coach probably would not have let us leave until we signed letters of intent to attend and run cross-country and track. She didn't, and we didn't.

After a tour of the campus, we drove to the beach. I walked out on the sand and stared east. I knew Africa lay on the other side of the Atlantic. That made me feel connected to my homeland, while still being close enough to my new home for my mom and dad to drive down and visit. Syracuse was only nine hours away. That may seem like a long distance to some people, but not me. Norfolk State was the closest warm school I could find. I planned on staying there four years and leaving with my degree. Because I chose not to sign a letter of intent, I did not have a scholarship. Instead, I took out federal loans to pay for my school myself. To me, this was an investment in my future.

I chose not to run cross-country my first semester at school. Like I said, my grades and test scores in high school left something to be desired. My grades weren't too bad considering I did not speak English when I arrived in New York in late July 2001. Still, I graduated high school on time in May 2004, just as my mom told me I would. All things considered, I felt very good about how far I'd come. However, I knew college presented a whole new set of challenges. Mom and Dad and I discussed it at great length and concluded I should not run right away so that I could adjust to the academic demands of college. I planned on running in the Olympics in 2008, but I had to take care of first things first. And that meant preparing to graduate college on time. Mom made sure of that.

Even though I did not go out for the cross-country team, I trained harder than I ever had. That was how I met one of the senior track stars for Norfolk, Tom Hightower. Tom and I hit it off immediately. He reminded me of my friends back in Kakuma, and he took care of Dominic and me the same way the older boys took care of the younger in the camp. The three of us ran down to the beach together nearly every day. When I run, I talk, and I told Tom about my big, Olympic dreams. He had to be a little skeptical when I first told him. After all, here I was, a freshman with the build of a football player who claimed to be a runner, a runner who didn't even go out for the cross-country team. He was a senior and one of the top runners at the school. Yet, it did not take long for him to see the potential in me.

One day, Tom and I were hanging out in his apartment, eating pizza. "In two years I can apply for citizenship," I told him, "and two years after that I am going to try out for the United States Olympic team."

"I believe you. I think you can do it. But, if you want to run in the Olympics, Norfolk isn't the right place for you."

That was not what I expected to hear. As a senior leader of the cross-country and track teams, he should have pressed me to go out for the team. Instead he told me to leave. "What are you talking about?" I asked.

"You are better than this place." Tom could tell from the look on my face that I still did not understand. "Lopez, you are an exceptional runner. You have more natural ability than anyone I have ever seen. But natural ability alone is not enough. There are a lot of good runners out there who never live up to their full potential. You need to go to a school that can teach you to get the most out of yourself."

"Where do you think I should go?"

"Northern Arizona University in Flagstaff, Arizona. The school sits at a high altitude, which helps distance runners. I spent a summer out there training with their coach. He knows his stuff. He can get you to the Olympics."

I didn't know much about Arizona beyond the fact that it was hot and far from home. "Let me think about it," I said.

"I'll contact the coach and tell him about you. Also, because you didn't go out for the team here this year, you still have all four years of eligibility left. That also means you won't have to sit out a year when you transfer."

"Don't call Arizona's coach. I can reach my dreams here. You and I can train together. That will be enough. You will see."

"No it won't, Lopez. I'm not as fast as you. You need to go up against guys who can really stretch you. You need to go to Northern Arizona."

Tom made a lot of sense, but I had something more to consider. Mom and I had found Norfolk State together. Plus, Dominic loved it here. He didn't want to transfer to Northern Arizona. The two of us had been inseparable since before he came to live with us. I was not sure I could leave without him. I also did not know how I could possibly tell Mom that I planned on transferring.

I didn't need to worry. When I broke the news to her that I was even considering transferring, she smiled and said, "Joseph, I don't care where you go to college, as long as you get your degree. That's all that matters to me." As for Dominic, both of us knew that eventually we had to go our own paths. Whether we shared an apartment in Norfolk or lived three thousand miles apart, we remained brothers. Nothing could change that.

But it was not as simple as that. The coach at Norfolk State did a little research when he saw Dominic and me running around the area. When he discovered our high school records, he wanted both of us on the cross-country and track teams. That summer, after our freshman year, he started recruiting us hard. I was back home in Syracuse talking to Mom and Dad when the coach called. Mom answered the phone. The coach must have figured he could make more progress with her than me, because he did his best to sell her on Norfolk State for both Dominic and me. "I have a full scholarship for Lopez," he said. "No more school loans, no more worrying about how to pay for school. Everything will be taken care of," he said.

Mom listened to what he had to say but was noncommittal. "It's up to you, Joseph," she told me. "You have to do what you think is right."

I was torn. I had not even seen Northern Arizona University yet. I'd talked to the cross-country and track coach there, Coach Hayes, and he wanted me on the team. However, my math scores were not yet high enough to qualify for a scholarship at NAU. I had to take, and pass, another math class before he could commit anything to me.

I didn't have to do anything more to qualify for a scholarship at Norfolk State. All I had to do was sign on the bottom line. I liked the school. I loved the weather. And I loved living next to the ocean. Arizona sat in the middle of the desert. Scenery wise, it could not compete with Norfolk.

The Norfolk coach called again the next day. Mom answered the phone. "Joseph, he wants an answer."

"Tell him to give me five minutes. I need to go pray," I said.

Five minutes didn't give God much time to give me an answer, but I knew He already had a plan for my life. He was the One who gave me my gifts and my dreams, and He was the one who brought me to America. "Oh God, hear my prayers. Let my cry come to You," I prayed. "I need to know what You want me to do, and I need to know it fast."

Five minutes later the phone rang. Mom again answered the phone. "Just a minute," I heard her say. She came into the living room where I was on my knees, praying. "What's it going to be?" she asked.

"Tell him to give my scholarship to someone else. I'm going to Northern Arizona University. That is the place that will take me to the Olympics."

Mom looked shocked by my answer. "What if you don't get into school there?"

"Don't worry. God wants me to go there."

"Dominic wants to stay at Norfolk State."

"All I can say to him is, 'Enjoy.' I am going to Northern Arizona."

"Are you sure?" I could tell from her voice that she was worried.

"Yes, Mom. I'm sure. It will be okay. You will see."

Mom smiled a nervous smile. "And you will get your degree," she said.

I laughed. "Yes, and my degree," I said. Northern Arizona might be the place that would take me to the Olympics, but it had also better be the place that took me to a degree. After all, that was the point of going to college, and I knew my mom would not let me forget it. Ever.

SEVENTEEN

Running for Joy

I trotted around the track, warming up. The stands were full. CBS Sports cameras covered every angle of the track. I should have been nervous, but I was not. A few months earlier I faced the pressure of an NCAA championship final race when I won the 3,000 meter indoor. I was not nervous then, and I was not now. Coach Hayes walked over to me. "How do you feel, Lopez?"

I grinned. "Great. This is really fun," I said.

Coach Hayes shook his head with a wide smile on his face. He assumed I had butterflies flopping around in my stomach. I didn't. Not even close. "Remember, this is a tactical race," he said. "You're going up against a really strong field. Most of these guys specialize in the 1500, so you have to run smart out there."

"Sure, Coach," I said. "No problem." Unlike my competitors, I did not have much experience in the 1500 but I had proven myself as a strong runner and we had a plan going into this race. The previous track season I ran the 800 almost exclusively. This season, I ran a little bit of everything, including the 800, relays, an occasional 400, and the 4-by-400 relay. Coach Hayes let me try all kinds of races to help me figure out which event best suited my skill set. I also volunteered for anything I could do to help the team score points.

Toward the end of the season, I ran the 1500 in a dual meet and in the conference meet. After running ten kilometers during the cross country season and 3,000 meters in the indoor track season, 1,500 meters seemed short. I liked the race because it requires more than pure speed or sheer endurance. You need both, plus you have to think all the way around the track for all four laps. Coach was right. The 1500 is a tactical race, which is why I entered it in the NCAA championships.

Because of my inexperience, I came in as a dark horse. No one knew what to expect from me in this event. Everyone, from the other teams to the fans to the media covering the event, seemed shocked when I zipped through the heats and semis to make it to the finals. Not me. I like this event. I expected great things from myself in it.

"Remember what I told you," Coach said. "Don't take off chasing the rabbit at the front of the pack. You need to save as much as you can for your kick in the last 80 to 90 meters. But don't get so obsessed over saving energy that you fall too far behind." He pulled off his ball cap and rubbed his head. He wanted to see me succeed as much as I did. "It's all about tactics, Lopez. You have to run strategically."

I smiled and said, "Yes, Coach, I understand. Don't worry. I've got this."

"Okay," he said. "I'll let you get back to warming up."

I lay down on the infield to stretch my legs, first the right, then the left. I looked around at the guys I would soon run against. The field looked very different than the one I ran against in my first "race" in the United States. It was more a fun run than a race because it took place at my dad's company picnic. The day's festivities included a 10K run. I never thought about entering until Dad said, "Come on. You should run." I did not have running shoes with me. "Here, use these," Dad said as he pulled off some generic running shoes for me to wear. They did not fit right. I hated running in shoes back then. They made my feet feel slow and heavy. But everyone who entered got a free T-shirt, and Mom promised me a Coke at the finish line. I couldn't say no to free T-shirts and Cokes, so I ran. Back then, that's all it took for me to run. It doesn't take much more today.

Running in that August heat and humidity took its toll. I nearly stopped halfway through, except my mom cheered me on. "You can do this, Joseph!" I finished third or fourth against an experienced field of runners, which wasn't bad for a soccer player.

Now I found myself in Sacramento, California, on a blistering hot June day. Some athletes complain about the heat, but I love it. The air was hot and dry, no humidity at all, just like Kakuma. Every day there was the same, with temperatures at or above 100 degrees; dry, hot air swirling around; zero humidity. My mind went back to running thirty kilometers around the perimeter of the camp without shoes, wearing ragged hand-me-down clothes. Back then I didn't even pause to grab a drink of water after finishing my lap around the camp; I was too eager to get into the soccer game. I would never think of doing that today. "Stay hydrated," Coach Hayes preached to the team. I could hear his voice in my head as I pulled out my water bottle and took a long drink.

"First call for the 1500," the loudspeakers announced. I gathered my things and walked toward the start line. Outside I put on my game face. Sunglasses on, stern look of determination on my face, I looked ready to dominate. Inside, I wore a huge grin. How could I not smile? Although this was the biggest race of my life up to this point, I did not run for my life. I ran that race a long time ago when I took off in the night with my three angels. We knew the rebel soldiers might open fire at any moment, which made us run even faster. Once we arrived in Kakuma, I ran every day, not just to play soccer but to take my mind off of my empty stomach and the harsh realities of life in the refugee camp. Today I ran for pure, absolute joy. My past set me free to enjoy the present moment, and I planned to enjoy it to the fullest. No man ever felt so blessed by God as I did in that moment.

"Second call, 1500 meters." My eleven competitors gathered near the start line. This was a strong field. Both the defending 1,500 meter out-door champion, Vincent Rono, and Leonel Manzano, the Mile indoor champion, made the final. Any one of half a dozen guys could easily win this race. I had to run smart.

I pulled off my warm-up jacket and pants and tossed them to Coach Hayes.

"You ready for this?" he asked.

"Yep," I said. I looked down at my navy blue jersey and the yellow letters across my chest: Northern Arizona University. Tom Hightower told me this place and Coach John Hayes would take me to the Olympics, and he knew what he was talking about. But over the past couple of years, NAU had grown to much more than that.

When I arrived on campus, I found they had one of the best hotel management programs in the country. God planted the idea of majoring in this area back when I got a part-time job at a local Best Western near my home in Tully. My goal then, and now, is to build a hotel in South Sudan and help open the area to tourists. Tourists bring money, and money will allow my people to build schools and hospitals and dig water wells. My success as an athlete can also help make these things happen. The lost boys of Sudan made the news back in 2001, but people have short memories. The more successful I am as an athlete as a former lost boy, the more people will talk about where I came from and the greater focus I can put on the needs of South Sudan. Then, with my education from NAU, I can lead the way in doing something.

None of this made me feel greater pressure as I lined up for the 1,500 meter final. Pressure is trying to make a UN food allotment stretch for thirty days. Pressure is watching friends die of malaria and wondering who in the camp will be next. Pressure is writing an essay that will determine your entire future in a language you do not know. A footrace, even a championship race, did not make me feel pressure.

"Third and final call for the 1500. Runners to the line," the loud-speakers announced. I stepped up to the start line in the sixth position, right in the middle of the field. Coach warned me to watch my position on the track throughout the race. "Don't let those guys box you in," he told me over and over again. The 1500, like every race longer than 400 meters, does not have lane assignments. If you are not careful, you can easily find yourself trapped on the inside, back in the pack, unable to maneuver. I planned to run a careful race.

"Runners, take your mark." I took a deep breath. *Enjoy*, I reminded myself.

The gun sounded. I took off, five guys inside of me, six outside. Everyone descends toward the middle of the track before the first turn. I didn't worry too much about running out too fast. The first lap of the 1500 doesn't count for anything. Rabbits sprint to an early lead, but they never last. *"Relax, relax, relax,"* I could hear the voice of Coach Hayes in my head. *"Run loose, not tight,"* he preached to me. If I were any looser, my legs would give out from under me.

We rounded the first turn at a pace I liked. The leader did not take off like a rabbit, nor did he hold back and make the race too slow. The rest of the field takes its cues from the leader. Coach Hayes was right when he said this is a tactical race. All races are, to some degree, even the ten kilometers of cross-country. In my first season at NAU I did not understand race strategy. I just went out and ran as hard as I could for as long as I could. My approach worked most of the season, but not when the team needed me the most. At the Big Sky Conference cross-country meet my first year, Coach told me to keep pace with Seth Pilkington, Weber State's top runner. Weber State and NAU went back and forth as the top team in the conference. Apparently, Seth's coach told him the same thing about me. The two of us ran the first seven kilometers so fast that neither of us scored any points for our squads. My team won the conference title, but I beat myself up over my foolish race. The next season I came back a different runner. Coach Hayes and that race finally convinced me that strategy means as much as speed. My second season also convinced Coach that the Olympic dream I talked about nonstop was a real possibility.

I trotted along through the first lap, right in the middle of the pack. The leader ran the first lap in just over fifty-eight seconds. I ran it in sixty. *Okay, a good, honest pace. I like this. This feels good*, I thought.

Before the first turn of the second lap, I sped up, moving from sixth to fourth. My place overall did not matter as much as the distance I wanted to keep between myself and the leader. The second lap is all about positioning yourself. No one has ever won the race on the second lap, but many have lost it there. If I let the leader stray too far from me, I would not be able to catch him at the end, no matter how strong my kick. And I had a very strong kick because I run a variety of distances. Most runners specialize, but I don't. I won the Big Sky Conference cross-country title in both 2006 and 2007, running 8,000 meters. Then, in 2006, I finished fourth in the NCAA outdoor track 800 meter race. My experience at so many different distances made me believe in my kick even more.

I settled into fourth position, keeping myself close to the leader. If he'd sprinted out from the pack, I would have moved up. But he stayed at a steady pace, and I matched him stride for stride. The track felt hot beneath my feet. Through the years I'd run on many different surfaces, from the jungle, to the savannah, where thorn bushes tore into my legs, to the sand and rocks under my bare feet in the camp. Back in high school, the track team ran through the school halls when it was too cold and snowy to run outside. I didn't so much run as bounce. Every other stride I jumped up to try to touch the ceiling. One day I didn't notice the door frame right in front of me. Next thing I knew I was in the nurse's office with no idea how I got there. Mom showed up, scared to death. "Joseph, from now on you need to focus on running straight, not jumping and running!"

I did not plan on doing any jumping or bouncing today, but I still planned on having fun. *Relax and enjoy this moment*, I reminded myself. I stayed just to the outside of the runner in third, leaving myself plenty of room to maneuver in case someone in front of me tripped and fell. I did not want someone else's mistake to take me down.

Back in Flagstaff, I had lots of people who went out of their way to keep me from tripping over myself. Professor Hales, my academic adviser, had me come into his office anytime I found myself getting frustrated under my class load. He sounded a lot like my mom. "You can do this," he told me over and over. Then he helped me plot a strategy to get through whatever had me overwhelmed. One of my Hotel Restaurant Management professors, Wally Rande, took me under his wing. He made sure I understood the material. He and Professor Hales used to listen to me go on about my crazy dreams of going to the Olympics and building a resort in South Sudan. Most important, they kept me on course. They became my family in Flagstaff. I could not have survived there without them.

I crossed the start line and began lap three, the lap where you put yourself in position to strike. We went along at a minute-a-lap pace for the first couple of laps, which is very fast but not too fast to maintain. I stayed less than half a second behind the leader. Fatigue starts to build in the third lap. Feet grow heavy. Legs weaken. I stayed focused on running my race. I ran relaxed over the first two laps. I kept myself in a safe position, avoiding the bunch-ups that often come in these races. Now I prepared my mind to strike. I thought back to watching Michael Johnson run in the 2000 Olympics. Head steady, arms pumping, legs flying. *Today is my day*, I told myself. *Run your race, and you will win.*

I stayed loose but focused through the third lap. We crossed the start line. A bell rang out. The first lap does not matter. The second lap is all about positioning. Lap three is when you prepare to strike. And lap four? Lap four is "Help me, God!"

Right into the curve we ran. *Wait for it . . . wait for it . . .* I told myself. The leader through the first three laps started to fade. Leo Manzano, the 1,500 meter indoor champion, moved into the lead. He'd run in the second position on laps two and three, with me right behind him. He sped up. I quickened my pace to stay close. I felt someone moving up on my outside shoulder. I moved out just enough to keep myself from getting boxed in.

Just a little bit more, I said to myself as we moved toward the back straightaway. Up ahead was the three hundred meter mark. The moment my feet crossed it, I started my kick. I darted into second. Up ahead, Leo Manzono sprinted hard. My legs felt strong through the final curve. "Save your energy for the final one hundred meter sprint," Coach had told me. We came out of the curve. The crowd roared, but I did not hear them. All I could hear was the rush of the wind past my ears and my heart banging in my chest.

I pushed myself as hard as I could. Manzano pushed himself as well. Fifty meters to go. He stayed one step ahead of me. I sprinted with everything within me. I moved to the outside. At the thirty meter mark I pulled nearly even with Manzano. A dead heat. At twenty meters I pulled just ahead. I never saw him again. Head up, eyes focused on the finish line, I ran as hard as I had ever run in my life for the win. I cruised through the finish line, took a few steps, punched the stopwatch on my wrist, then collapsed on the track in joy. I looked up at the heavens and made the sign of the cross. "Thank You, God. Thank You. May You multiply this gift You have given me more and more." My prayer had to do with far more than running.

I got up and shook Leo Manzano's hand. "Great race," he said.

"You too." The third place finisher came over and shook my hand as well.

A CBS television camera came over to me. I could hardly contain my excitement. Now I understood why Michael Johnson cried after winning the Olympic gold in his last race. "Lopez, congratulations. You ran an incredible race," the reporter said.

"Thank you," I said. Then I looked into the camera and said, "I told you, Mom. Thank you for the opportunity."

Far away, in a living room in Tully, New York, my mom wept. We shared this moment even though we were thousands of miles apart.

Later I learned that four runners in my final finished with times under 3:38. For a collegiate race, that is a blistering pace.

After my championship race, the United States Track Team invited me to run for the United States in the Pan American Games in Rio, Brazil. I could represent the United States because a couple of weeks after the NCAA Championships another dream came true: I became a United States citizen on July 4, 2007. However, I decided not to run in the Pan Am Games. Someone else contacted me with a better offer, one for which I had waited seventeen years.

EIGHTEEN

Family Reunion

I saw my biological mother for the first time since I was six while sitting in my dorm at Northern Arizona University. My friend Melissa Kiehlbaugh had just returned from another of her trips to Kenya. She and I got to know one another a year earlier when Melissa approached me in the student union and asked if I was from Kenya. At the time, I was a little suspicious. Who was this little white girl who came up and started talking to me out of the blue? Then she spoke a few words in Swahili, and I was like, *Who is this little white girl?*

Melissa and I became fast friends. That first day I told her my story, including details about my biological mother and father. By this time my mother lived in Kenya with my brothers I had never met, Peter and Alex. My mom and dad in New York sent my parents money every month, which allowed my brothers to go to school in Kenya. On her last trip to Kenya, Melissa took photographs of me to show my mother. And while she was there, she took pictures of my mother for me.

That is how I was able to see my mother after all those years, while sitting in my dorm room in Flagstaff, Arizona. Melissa opened up her laptop, clicked a few buttons, and there was a familiar face I did not remember. I ran over to the mirror and looked closely at myself. I could see my mother in me! I hugged Melissa so tight that her eyes nearly popped out of her head. "You are now my sister," I said. "You brought my mother back to me. I've heard her voice, but now I can see her! That makes you more than a friend. It makes you my sister."

Two years later my phone rang. "This is Mary Carillo with HBO's *Real Sports*," a woman said. "Our producers watched you win the 1500 in the NCAA Championships and were intrigued by your story. We would like to do a feature on you, if you are interested."

"Of course, yes. Thank you," I said. Anytime anyone asked me to tell my story, I accepted the offer. Running gave me a platform to talk about South Sudan and the lost boys. I had to use it. I assumed a crew from HBO would fly out to Arizona, ask a few questions, and shoot some footage of me running. Mary Carillo had something much bigger in mind.

A few weeks after the initial phone call, I boarded a plane in Phoenix bound for New York's JFK Airport. It was the same airport into which I'd flown six years earlier when I came to America from Kenya. Mary met me at the airport along with one of her producers. The three of us boarded a plane bound for London. I used my new United States passport for the very first time. While that may not sound like a big deal to most people, it was to me. The last time I boarded a plane in JFK, I was a lost boy carrying a bag of papers and no luggage. Now I flew as a very proud American. In London we boarded another plane. Eight hours later I walked off a Jetway and into a place I had not seen in six years. We were back in Kenya. Mary Carillo and HBO planned to take me to meet my mother.

Although I wanted to see my mother as quickly as possible, after twenty hours of travel across eleven time zones, I needed a good night's sleep first. A film crew was to meet with us in the morning and take us to my mother's house. HBO put me in a nice hotel for the night, much nicer than the dorm at the Boys' Center in Juja where I lived for six months.

Back then I thought Nairobi had to look and sound and smell just like America. Now I knew better.

My mind raced when I lay down and tried to sleep. No one told my mother I was coming to see her. She would not know until I walked in her door. Lying in the dark, the sounds of Nairobi echoing outside, I wondered how she would react when she saw me. The first time we talked, she did not believe it was me because I was no longer a little boy. Melissa showed her photographs of me on her last visit. I knew my mother did not expect to see a little boy any longer. However, I did not know what she would think of me, her long-lost son.

I also thought of the rest of my family I'd left behind so long ago. My two brothers, Abraham and John, and my sister, Susan, still lived in Sudan. After I was kidnapped, my parents hid them in caves at night to protect them from the rebel soldiers. My parents, along with all the other parents in the area, stopped bringing their children to church, or practically anywhere else. If rebels wanted large groups of children to take all at once, they had to look elsewhere. My dad also remained in Sudan. He worked the farm to provide for the family, while my mother stayed with Peter and Alex in Juja. When I was a boy, only the wealthiest families sent their children to Kenya for school. Now my family was wealthy, thanks to the $200 my American family sent them every month. Long ago that seemed like a great deal of money.

Morning came. The camera crew arrived. I was up early, waiting for them. The day felt like my birthday, Christmas, the Fourth of July, and every other holiday all rolled into one. "This has to be what Joseph felt like the day his father arrived from Canaan," I told the camera crew. Like me, Joseph in the Old Testament was taken away from his family as a boy. He endured years of hardship, first as a slave then in a prison. Everyone assumed he was dead. Later, God not only set him free but showed him that He planned to use all the bad that had happened to him for good. God did the same thing for me. Years after he received his new life, Joseph had a family reunion with his father whom he never thought he would see again. Now I knew exactly how Joseph felt. The two of us were connected by more than a name.

We loaded into a Toyota Land Rover and drove from the hotel to Juja, eighteen miles away. On my first trip to Juja in 2001, I thought it was a very nice, modern place. In comparison to Kakuma, it was. My American eyes saw it very differently. My mother's neighborhood has no electricity and no running water. Women walked down the street carrying five-gallon jerricans filled with water. Later I learned all the water had to be boiled before it could be used for anything.

A few blocks from my mother's apartment house, people took notice of our vehicle. Americans always create a stir in Juja, especially Americans flanked by camera crews. The driver slowed down as a group of children ran toward our car. "Wait a minute!" I said. "I recognize those boys. Stop the car." The car stopped. Children jumped on the running boards and reached into the windows. I leaned out and called over to two boys standing just to the side of the road. "I know you," I said. "You are my brothers!" I motioned for them to come over to me. They did, but I could tell from the looks on their faces they had no idea what was going on. They came because of the television cameras, not because of me. I didn't care. I knew who they were, and that was enough. I leaned out the window and pulled one over close to me. "How are you doing, buddy? I'm your brother, Lopez." My brothers did not speak English. I am sure they wondered who this crazy American was, although our mother had a photograph of me that I was sure the boys had seen.

I jumped out of the car. Mary followed. "These are my brothers, Peter and Alex," I said.

"Nice to meet you," Mary said. The two boys stayed close to me, but not too close. They were still unsure of exactly who or what I was.

We were close enough now to my mother's apartment that I decided to walk. Cameramen walked backward in front of me as if I were some sort of big celebrity. Mary and the HBO producer fell in behind me. The farther we walked, the more the buzz around us grew. Children ran to their houses, then came back dragging along their parents. Soon we had a full parade moving down the dirt streets near where my mother lived.

I turned a corner. The street became much narrower. Houses built of mud bricks rose up on either side. People danced along beside me. Word was out: the lost boy had come home! The dead boy was back from the grave. The party had started already.

The parade stopped. The sea of people around me parted. All eyes turned to the woman standing in a doorway. That's when I saw her. "Mama," I called out to the face I recognized from Melissa's photographs. I'd stared at that photograph so long and so close that I knew every line. "Mama, it's me, Lopez."

"Lopepe!" she screamed. I rushed over to her, but her friends and relatives got in my way. I hugged her friends while pushing my way to my mother. She reached up to me and hugged me tight around my neck. Seventeen years had passed since the soldier ripped me out of her arms, seventeen very long years in which we'd both given up on one another as dead.

"Here, here, here," she called out in Buya. She took out some fermented flour and sprinkled it around my neck in a circular motion. In Sudan, this ceremony expresses great joy. I kneeled down to make it easier for her to reach my neck. All around us, people clapped and cheered.

"What's going through your mind right now?" Mary asked me.

"I'm speechless," I said. "I mean, this is my family . . . unbelievable." When I was a small boy alone in Kakuma, I dreamed of this moment. I soon found I had to give up this dream if I was to survive life in the refugee camp. Still, a faint hope that my mother and father might someday come and find me never completely went away. When they never did, I assumed they were dead. I looked up at my mother and tried to memorize the scene. I never wanted to forget this resurrection moment. I dreamed of this day, and now my dream had come true.

My mother finished the flour ceremony. She jumped up and ran out into the crowd. I watched as she jumped up and down and did the Sudanese call of joy. "Aiee, aiee, aiee, aiee," she sang as she hopped up and down several times. Then she turned around in a circle three times, her hand on the back of her head. Finally, she charged over to me and pulled me into a tight embrace one more time. This was her dance of joy.

The crowd on the street grew even larger. My mother pulled me into the house and back into the apartment. The crowds stayed outside. People stood at the window and looked in. My mother and I went into the small apartment bedroom, adobe walls around us, a concrete floor beneath us. I sat down next to my mother. Other relatives crowded into the room near us. I sat there, staring at her and she at me. I tried to speak, but no words could come out. Instead, sixteen years of emotion spilled out of me. The two of us sat there, holding one another, crying both tears of joy for the moment and sorrow for the years we'd lost. My Sudanese mother and her American son reunited at long last. "*Katali, katali, katali*," she repeated over and over again. That is, "happy, happy, happy." I felt the same way.

Later that day I broke out another surprise for my family. I showed them my race from the NCAA championships on a portable DVD player. Televisions were no more common for my family than they were for me when I lived in Kakuma. A television so small was unbelievable to them. They gathered around as I started the race footage. I gave them a play-by-play in Swahili. CBS's American commentators did not make much sense to my mother, brothers, aunts, and uncles. Throughout the entire race, my mother patted her chest with her right hand. When I passed Manzano with twenty meters to go, she raised her arms in the air. When I crossed the finish line to win the race, she smiled from ear to ear. Then she heard a word on the screen she understood quite well. In the interview immediately after the race, I said, "Mom, thank you for this opportunity."

"For you, Mother," I said. She hugged me tight. My words made tears flow down the faces of two mothers on opposite sides of the world.

When evening came, I went back to my hotel in Nairobi. My mother did not want to let me go. "I will return in the morning," I told her. She grabbed hold of me and hugged me so tight I thought a bone might break. "I promise, Mother, tomorrow. I will see you again tomorrow. I do not go back to America for two weeks." Reluctantly, she let me go.

The next day HBO had a surprise for me. My father arrived at my mother's home. HBO flew him from Sudan to Nairobi just to see me. He'd never been on an airplane before. Like me, he finally got to ride in one of the planes the two of us used to watch fly far overhead. Looking at my father was like looking at the future me in a mirror. We embraced in the street. Then my father looked at me and asked, "Where did you come from?"

I laughed. "Far away in America." I knew he did not understand. When you have lived in the same small corner of the world your entire life, you assume everywhere is nearby. He must have wondered why it had taken me so long to come home. After all, we'd talked on the phone for four years now. America must be very far away if it took me four years to return from there. It took most of the two weeks I was there just to explain how I had to go back to America. Both my mother and father expected me to stay with them forever.

Once I convinced them I had unfinished work I had to do in America, my father said to me, "I know you are with good people now. You are safe. So I will let you return to America, but first we have some unfinished work of our own we must complete."

The dream I found myself in was about to become even more surreal. I was about to go home.

NINETEEN

Back from the Grave

My father had unfinished business in our home village. I had a plane to catch. "I must show the village you are alive," he said. "And I must make you alive again." My Buya was very rusty. I did not fully understand the second part of what he said. I tried to talk him out of his plan, but he refused to take no for an answer. It wasn't that I did not want to see my home village. I did, very much, but I didn't think I had enough time to go all the way to Kimotong, then make it back to Nairobi before my flight home.

"I only have a couple of days for the extra trip. Can we make it in that time?" I asked. My question showed how American I had become. I came from the land of clocks and calendars and schedules that must be kept, none of which meant anything to my father. "How long?" I asked.

"Not long," my father replied.

"I have to get back in time to catch my plane back to America."

"No problem," my father said.

I should have known better than to have listened.

HBO flew my father down from Kimotong to meet me in Juja. However, the producers went back to New York before my father insisted I go back to our village. I was a college student who lived on Ramen noodles and peanut butter and jelly between semesters. I could not afford to charter a plane back to Kimotong.

"No problem," my father said. He'd made this trip many times and knew what to do.

The next day I found myself wedged between my parents on a seat made for two in the back of a packed-out Kenyan bus. Three and some-times four people wedged themselves into each seat, many of whom had their farm animals right beside them. Behind me, a family laid a two-by-four across the center aisle to create extra seating for their children. Chickens weaved between the children's legs, clucking and roaming up and down the aisle. No child could fit down the packed aisle, much less an adult. The goats not lucky enough to find a seat inside the bus were strapped to the roof between the boxes and baskets that passed as lug-gage in Kenya. Even with the windows open, no air moved inside the crowded bus. Dust filled any empty space. The farther north we drove into the desert, the hotter and dustier it got. I could hardly breathe.

The bus rocked from side to side as it navigated between washed-out portions of road. My legs ached from the cramped space. I squirmed, trying to get comfortable. My stomach growled; my tongue stuck to the roof of my mouth. I glanced at my parents. The trip was pure luxury for them. They were accustomed to walking everywhere. A bus ride felt like first-class accommodations for them.

Day turned into night. Night turned into day. We stopped very infre-quently for food and water. More people packed the bus at each stop. A few got off, but it felt like more always got on.

After forty-eight hours on the bus, we arrived at the town of Kakuma near the Sudanese border. The nearby camp where I spent ten years got its name from the town. "How much farther?" I asked. I knew the answer.

"Not far," my father said. He was accustomed to walking from here to our village. I did not have time for that. I found a place to rent a car in Kakuma and hired a driver and a bodyguard to take us the rest of the way.

Six hours later we pulled into Kimotong, my boyhood home of which I had no memories. I climbed out of the car and into a celebration that began before we got there. I do not know how everyone knew we were on our way, but they did. My sister stood in the middle of the crowd. I did not know her until she introduced herself. People seemed glad to see me, but they kept their distance. I did not understand why. My father barked out directions, sending one person off to the fields to bring back my brother, instructing someone else to bring the animals for the sacrifice.

I started to step forward into the celebration, but my mother stopped me. "First we must cleanse the spirits," she said. I had no idea what she was talking about. My sister handed my mother an egg. Mother broke the egg and poured it out on the ground between us and the celebration. She and my father hurdled over the broken egg. "Do the same," she directed me. I did as I was told.

Once I hurdled the egg, the mob closed in on me with hugs and kisses. We went into a thatched roof hut next to the car. It looked vaguely familiar to me, like something out of a long-forgotten dream. A fireplace stood in the center, with a cooking area on one side, sleeping mats rolled up on the other. A ladder went up to a storage shelf above the cooking area. It seemed so small now compared to the giant house of my dreams. People crowded inside. "This is where you were born," my mother told me. The party in the hut this day had to be like the celebration they held on the day I was born. The son had come back from the dead.

Every few minutes I instinctively looked at my watch. I felt guilty every time I did. All around me people talked and laughed, oblivious to time and schedules. Time doesn't exist in Kimotong, at least not in the way it does in America. As much as I tried to savor the experience, I found myself torn between the excitement of the moment and the knowledge that I had a plane to catch. We'd traveled nearly three days to get here. I did not know how I would get back to Nairobi in time for my flight. *Don't worry about it. You'll get there. This trip is a miracle from God. Enjoy it,* I told myself over and over. Next thing I knew, I was looking at my watch again.

Two hours after we arrived, my long-lost brother John walked through the door. I knew he had to be my brother, but I did not recognize him. The moment John walked in, the celebration started all over again. Someone else walked in and whispered something to my father. "Follow me," he said to me.

The two of us walked out onto the path in front of the hut. A group of men came up to us, leading a white goat. They were the village elders. One of the elders took out a knife and slit the goat's throat. The goat fell to the ground. The elder then took his knife and made a long cut from the goat's chest to the bottom of the stomach. Everything the goat had eaten over the past few days spilled out onto the ground. The smell . . . I cannot describe it. My American stomach nearly emptied. The elder then scooped up a large handful of the goat's stomach contents and smeared it across my chest. My stomach wrenched at the smell. Before I knew what had just happened, he took another handful and smeared it down my stomach, then onto my arms and legs. Thankfully I wore jeans instead of the shorts I wore the day I went to my mother's apartment in Juja.

The crowd that was gathered around us seemed relieved by the elders' actions. Apparently, smearing goat guts over a person bestows a great blessing on the smearee while also driving away any evil spirits. Judging by the amount of goat guts smeared on me, I was very, very blessed. I waved my hand over the goat guts. "How long?" I asked.

"Sundown," my father said. I had to stay like this until the sun went down for me to get the full effect. The guts soaked through my T-shirt. I didn't think I could wait until sundown to wash, but I had no choice. The elders took what remained of the goat over to the women. They quickly butchered it. The village feasted on goat that day. It was a rare treat for them all. Livestock is very valuable. People eat meat very rarely.

In spite of the guts and smell, people flocked around me. Rapid-fire questions flew at me. I could not understand what anyone said to me. I felt like I did when I first arrived in America. My Buya now was on the same level my English was back then. Even though my mother and I spoke every week, she now spoke Swahili. Living in Kenya, she had to learn it to get by. I'd held onto my Swahili, but not Buya beyond a handful of words. Thankfully a new person came into the village. Clement came down from Juba, which is now the capital of the newly independent South Sudan, when he heard I was on my way back home. He worked for a mission organization, translating the Bible into Buya. Because he also spoke English, he became my translator for the trip.

"They want to know if you are really Lopepe," Clement said.

"Yes, yes. I am him."

"'Are you going to stay here?' they ask."

"No. I have to go back to America."

While Clement translated my answer, I looked closely at the children playing nearby. A very vague memory came back of making bulls and other animals out of mud. I tried to picture these kids in America, playing with LEGOs and video games. Instead, they were covered with dirt from head to toe. That was me, I told myself. I was that kid. I could barely make myself believe it. The village did not have a school. None of these kids would ever learn to read and write as long as they stayed here. Only a few lucky children, like my brothers Peter and Alex, got to go away to Kenya for an education, and they only had this opportunity because my American parents paid their way.

Sundown came. My sister went down to the river and brought back a bucket of water for me. I washed the goat guts off myself. That night I slept outside under the stars. There was not room for me in the hut.

The next morning I got up, expecting to drive back to Kenya. If I hurried, I should be able to catch my plane. My father, however, had other ideas. What I thought had been a celebration the day before was merely the warm-up for the main event. Even more people crowded into our village from the surrounding area. The church from which I'd been taken served villages from all around the area. My father sent word to all the villages which had lost children to come and celebrate with us. "One of the lost ones has returned from the grave," he said. Very few, if any, of those taken with me were ever seen again. My appearance gave all the other families hope that they, too, might one day have a child return from the dead.

My mother and father led me just outside the village to a small, fenced enclosure about the size of a backyard vegetable garden back in the States. Inside the short fence I saw piles of rocks lined up in an orderly fashion. We walked to a small pile of rocks in a far corner. A man stood nearby holding onto a white bull. The crowd from the village had followed us to the fenced area. They lined up just outside the fence, watching us. That's when it hit me. I was standing in the village cemetery. The pile of rocks in front of me was my grave.

My father turned to the crowd. Everyone fell silent. He started speaking. The translator told me what he said. "Many years ago, my son was taken from us. We thought he was dead. This is his grave. We buried what remained of him and mourned him for many days. But now, my son who was dead has come back to us again!" The crowd cheered. Many people wept.

The man with the bull then pulled out a long spear. Right there on top of my grave, he rammed the spear through the side of the bull. It dropped to the ground, dead. The blood soaked the ground. Just like the day before, the elders then split open the bull's abdomen. I prepared myself for what I knew was coming next. The American in me did not want to have guts smeared on me again. The sight and the smell made my stomach queasy. Yet, as the boy who had returned from the grave, I very much wanted to do whatever it took to be alive again in my village. These were the traditions of my mother and father and my people. This ceremony was a part of who I am and who I will always be, no matter what country I call home. I nodded to the elder as if to say, "I'm ready." He scooped up a handful of the remains of the bull and rubbed it onto my arms and legs while the entire village looked on.

After the bull ceremony, my father took a spade and dug up my grave. Carefully, he pulled out a shirt and a pair of shorts, both ragged from the years in the ground. Then he removed a couple of toys and a belt of traditional beads. In Buya culture, these beads meant as much as a string of diamonds or pearls. I did not recognize the beads, but I knew they were valuable by the reaction of the crowd when my father lifted them up for all to see.

The elders took the bull away to be butchered and cooked. My father motioned for me to make a speech. I wanted to do as he asked, but I could not speak. The flood of emotions pouring over me choked the words out. My father did not understand why I stood there silently. "Speak," he said.

I choked back my tears. "Okay," I said to him. Every eye was on me. I paused to gather my thoughts. What do you say at your own gravesite when you come back from the dead? I thought for a moment, swallowed hard, then started. "I am very glad I am alive," I said in English. Clement translated. "I did not think I would ever see my family again. I thought they were dead. I survived in the refugee camp in Kenya. After many years, I went to the United States. It is very far away. You must go there by airplane." A buzz went up at that line. People pointed up in the air to one another, amazed that someone who had actually flown on one of the jets high overhead was actually in their midst.

"Do not give up on any of the kids who were taken with me. Do not forget them. God is great. Do not give up on life, and do not give up on Him. He can and will bring more of these kids back to you.

"I must return to the United States, where I currently attend university. I never thought I would have this opportunity, but God gave it to me. Now I must return to finish the work I started. I will return. Do not give up on anybody. God is great."

I could not say anything more. The crowd seemed surprised I spoke such a short time. In Africa, speeches stretch out for hours. Emotionally, I could not last hours. On top of that, I had a plane to catch and a very long journey in front of me to get to it.

The crowd made their way from the cemetery back to our house. I followed, answering questions along the way. The women cooked the bull. The celebration was just getting started. Again I looked at my watch. I could not stop myself. *Relax. You will get there when you get there. Hakuna matata—stop worrying.* I started to glance at my watch but stopped myself. This celebration was too important to rush.

The celebration of that day was tempered with sadness. Death is a daily reality in equatorial Africa. Medical care is very limited. Doctors and hospitals exist only in the large cities. Even the most basic medicines rarely make it to places like Kimotong. I came face-to-face with these limitations when a mother came to me, holding her little girl. The child appeared to be moments from death. The mother pleaded with me. I could not understand what she said.

"Medicine," my translator said. "The child has malaria and the mother wants you to give her medicine to make her well."

My heart broke. "Why does she think I have medicine?"

"Because you came here from America."

I began to weep. "Please tell her that I do not have the medicine she needs. I cannot do anything for her daughter." The translator told the mother. She did not move. She looked at Clement, then looked at me, desperate. Her eyes told me, *But you are my only hope.* Finally, she walked away, sad and dejected. The child did not survive the day. In the three days I was there, twenty-four children died. Several desperate mothers came to me, pleading with me to heal their children. "My child is vomiting and cannot stop. Can you help him?" I was asked multiple times. Sadly, I could do nothing. On the other side of the village, the celebration of my resurrection continued. I almost became angry. "Why am I celebrated when another life is taken by a disease so easily prevented?"

On the morning of the third day I pulled my father aside. "Father," I said, "I have no choice. I must go back today."

"No, no. One more day."

I shook my head. "No, Father. I must leave today. But I will come back. I promise."

He let out a long sigh. I took his hand. "My father, I give you my word. I will be back. Thank you for bringing me home again. Thank you for digging me out of the grave and for showing me life here. God wanted me to see my home again, but He also wants me to go back to America."

"Okay," he said.

After many tearful good-byes, I climbed into the rental car and headed back to Kenya. My mother and father came with me. Even after we left, the celebration in Kimotong continued. The party would not stop until the food ran out.

I rode along in the car, swaying from side to side from the deep ruts of the washed out road. My heart remained back in Kimotong. God opened my mind during that ride home. My life now came into focus. I had always wanted to use the platform my gifts gave me to make a difference in the lives of others, especially in my home country. Now I understood the depth of the needs there. I have to do something, I told myself. *Something* was a very broad term for a place where everything was needed. Schools, clean water, medicine, decent farming equipment, you name it, anything and everything could make a difference for my people. I knew I could not supply all these things by myself. *But where can I find help?* I wondered. *Where can I find others who care about my people as much as I do?*

The trip back to Juja took just as long as the trip to Kimotong. Saying good-bye to my mother and father was very difficult for all of us. Tears flowed freely. My mother clung to me. She did not want to let me go. "I will come back," I assured her.

"When?"

"December. Christmas. I promise."

"Wait, wait, wait," she said. "I must give you something to remember me by before you go."

"But my plane," I said.

"Wait," she said. She flew into a whirl of activity. A few minutes later she placed a woven ring in my hand. "I did not have any red beads, only yellow, black, and green. The yellow is supposed to be red. When you wear this, you will think of me."

I placed the ring on my finger. I have yet to take it off.

TWENTY

Running Down My Dream

I went back to Flagstaff after returning from Africa to get ready for the fall semester and the upcoming cross-country season. Most experts tagged our team at Northern Arizona as the team to beat in the Big Sky Conference after we won the conference title the year before. Even before our first practice, the team set its sights on a much larger goal. Winning the Big Sky Conference was nice, but we wanted to win the team national title at the NCAA championships at the end of the year in Terra Haute, Indiana. Personally, I wanted to win the individual national title not just for me but for the team as well. I loved my teammates at NAU. Running with them felt like running with my friends back in Kakuma. I would do anything for these guys.

Training began like it always did, with an overnight camping trip in the mountains above Flagstaff. We ran and played a lot of silly games that helped bond everyone together as a team. In the serious moments, I talked to the team about our goals for the season. And of course, we ran and ran some more. Running always gives me joy. When I run, I feel set free from the world.

But this season, something had changed. On long runs, my mind raced back to Kimotong. I saw the faces of the children as they played in the dirt. Here I was, working on my college degree, and those children had no hope of any kind of education. I felt guilty being here, even though I shouldn't. God gave me this opportunity. I had to take full advantage of it. Yet the more I reminded myself of this fact, the more I saw those little kids, playing in the dirt, without any hope of a better future.

I also saw the mothers who brought their children to me, desperate for help. No matter how hard I tried, I couldn't get that image out of my head. *I have to do something for them.* I knew God had not brought me this far for me alone. He did not give me the ability to run just for me to go out and win races or even to support my team. He had something much bigger planned. *God, help me know what to do*, I prayed as I ran.

The faces of my own family flashed in my mind as I ran. I closed my eyes and saw my mother and father, sister and brothers. My relationship with them changed after actually spending time with them. Talking on the phone, I knew this was my family and I loved them. But after spending two weeks in Africa with them, my heart ached for them. The money my American parents sent them each month made a tremendous difference in their lives, but I did not feel right about asking Mom and Dad to continue supporting my family. After Dominic, Peter, and I graduated and moved out, the Rogers brought in three more lost boys to live with them. Mom and Dad had done enough for me already. I needed to take over this responsibility myself, but how could I do that and remain in college?

The questions in my head grew louder and louder the closer I came to the start of the cross-country season. I knew I had to do something. I felt like it was time for me to turn pro. This wasn't the first time I'd considered becoming a professional track athlete. After I won the 1500 NCAA championship, reps from different shoe companies let me know in a roundabout way that they would be open to sponsoring me when and if I decided to turn pro. I talked to Coach Hayes at the end of the 2007 track season. He knew this might be a good time for me to go pro, but also knew how important it was for me to stand on the podium at the National Cross Country Championships with my NAU teammates. Nike really wanted me but I had an obligation to the team that had become my family. We decided that I would stay at least through cross country. Coach Hayes left NAU during the Summer to take the same position at the Air Force Academy. I trusted his judgment and stayed through Cross Country. The Olympic trials were coming up in June. Turning pro after the fall 2007 semester would set me free to train exclusively for the Olympics. "You can always negotiate to have your sponsors pay for your college so you can go back to school during the off season," he told me. I liked the sound of that. I wanted my degree, which is what made this decision so difficult.

I knew after making this decision that I had to make another phone call. I didn't want to call, but I knew I had to. I took a deep breath, dialed the number, and said a quick prayer while the phone rang.

"Hello," Mom said.

"Hi Mom, it's me, Lopez."

"Joseph, it's so good to hear your voice. Everything okay in Arizona?"

"Yes, everything is great. But I need to talk to you and Dad about something. Is he there?"

Mom paused. "Yeah, let me put him on the other line."

A few moments later he said, "What's going on, Lopez?"

My heart raced because I did not know how they would take my news. "I have decided to drop out of school and turn professional in track," I said. Before either of them could say anything, I added, "I only have three semesters of work left to finish my degree, which I can do during the off seasons. I give you my word that I will get my degree."

"Are you sure about this?" Mom asked.

I knew she was worried I would not reach the goal the two of us shared. "I will make sure any contract I sign has money set aside just for school. I promise. I will graduate; it will just take a little longer than I first planned."

Neither of my parents said anything for what felt like a long time. Finally Dad said, "You don't have to do this because of the money. You know that, don't you?"

"Dad, Mom, you have been great parents to me. You have given me so much. But now it is time for me to support myself and to support my family in Sudan."

"We—" my dad tried to interrupt.

"I have to do this," I said, "and now is the best time to do it. The Olympic trials are in June. If I am going to make the team, I need to start training full-time. Coach Hayes said I can work out with the Air Force Academy team. He's even going to let me live with him until I am able to move into the US Olympic training center in Colorado Springs."

Another long pause on the other end of the phone. "As long as you finish your degree, we support your decision 100 percent," Mom said.

"We can't wait to go to Beijing and watch you run," Dad added. He sounded excited. "You're going to make the team and we will be there to see it all!" I'd only talked about the Olympics for six and a half years. My dream had never been so close. Mom and Dad believed in my dream even more than I did, if that were possible.

Now that I'd made my decision, I had to break the news to my team-mates. "Guys, there's nothing I love more than running with you. But there's something I have to do. I am going to leave school and turn pro as soon as our season is over."

"You've got to do it to get ready for the Olympics, man," one guy said. "We understand."

"That's part of it," I said, "a big part."

Someone shouted from the back, "If I could run like you, I'd do the same thing. What are you waiting for?"

I laughed. "Thanks for understanding. The way I see it, if this is my last season, I plan on making it my best ever. I say we go out and win a national championship."

We almost reached that goal. At one point in the season, we were ranked second in the nation. I won the individual conference title, while our team won conference for the second year in a row. We qualified as a team for the national championships in Terra Haute. I finished third individually, while our team finished fourth overall. Our new coach, Eric Heins, was named Big Sky Conference Coach of the Year. I was even named the NCAA Mountain Region male track athlete of the year. Any way you look at it, 2007 was a very, very good season. I ended my collegiate career on a high note.

As soon as the cross-country season ended, I contacted Nike to tell them I was ready. Coach Hayes recommended an agent who negotiated the deal for me. I moved to Colorado Springs in early January after returning to Kenya for the second time to spend Christmas with my family.

The Air Force Academy had just returned from winter break when I arrived. I was a little nervous about training with a new group of guys, but Coach Hayes put my fears to rest. "You're going to love it here," he told me. "I know I do. These athletes are different from any I've ever been around. Don't get me wrong. We had a fantastic team at Northern Arizona, but there's just something about a team whose sole focus is on something much bigger than themselves. Their purpose for being here transcends sports. You'll see."

After one or two workouts, I knew exactly what he was talking about. I found myself drawn to the cadets' sense of purpose, ideals, and their sacrifice to serve the United States. I am a very proud American, but these guys had a deep love and pride for our country unlike I had ever encountered. Every day I came away from practice inspired.

Even though I was at the Academy as a guest of Coach Hayes, I quickly fell in with the team. Everyone here had a nickname. My friend Ian McFarland was Baby Mac, because everyone said he had a baby face. The team named Kevin Hawkins, who stood nearly seven feet tall and ran the 800 meter, "Carl," after the giant in the movie *Big Fish*. Kenneth Grosselin was Kenny G. He couldn't play the sax, but he finished at the top of his class. He inspired me both on and off the track. I already had a nickname, Lopez, so I fit right in with the guys. Before long, my new training partners felt like family, very much like my friends in Kakuma.

I dove into my training at the Academy. I came here to train without distractions. However, I never counted on a beautiful blonde distraction finding me. On the first day of hurdle drills, Coach Hayes and I stood to one side talking, when a sophomore cadet girl came right up to me. "Hello, my name is Brittany," she said with a huge smile. "Welcome to Colorado Springs."

I am a talker, but I get tongue-tied and shy around girls. I blurted out something like, "Hi, I'm Lopez."

"How do you like the Air Force Academy so far?" Her eyes danced. I could not believe this girl was talking to me!

Coach Hayes gave me a look and put his hand over his mouth to keep from laughing.

"I like it very nice," I said, or something that eloquent. I could not get over how happy and cheerful she was.

"Good. I love it here, and the track team is great. We're like a big family here. I'm sure we'll see lots of each other. I'm on the girls' team. Maybe we can run together sometime."

"Okay, yeah, sure. I would like that," I stammered.

"Well, it's nice to meet you. I'm glad you're here," she said before turning and running back to a group of girls. I watched her the whole way back. Immediately I felt myself falling for her.

Over the next few weeks I had more conversations with Brittany at practice. None of them were anything earthshaking, but I felt myself being drawn more and more to her. The problem was, I had no idea how to approach her to let her know how I felt. Back in Kakuma, I would have asked my family of boys for advice. In Colorado Springs, I went to the closest thing I had to my family back in the camp.

One day during practice, Baby Mac, Kenny G, and I were out on the track running laps. When I run, I talk, so I confided in them. "Guys, I think I'm falling for Brittany."

Kenny G laughed. "So you're going for a cadet, are you? Well, that didn't take long."

Baby Mac joined in. "So, the big, bad pro athlete gets his heart taken by a little blonde runner, huh?"

"Yeah, I guess so. What should I do?" I asked. "I don't know anything about girls and relationships."

"Who does?" Baby Mac laughed. "Just talk to her. Ask her out. You should go for it, man."

I listened to his advice, and I really wanted to follow it, but I could not bring myself to say the words, "Will you go out with me?" At the same time, I could not hide my feelings forever. I knew eventually they would come spilling out. I only hoped I wouldn't make a fool of myself when they did.

A few months later, after an especially hard workout together, I limped into the trainers' room for an ice bath. They call these things baths, but only because you immerse yourself in water while wearing athletic gear. The trainers' room is very cold and sterile anyway, like a medical facility. The ice baths make it that much colder. I hate the cold, and I hate ice baths even more. If not for the way they made my muscles heal, I would swear them off forever.

Both the men's and women's track teams share the trainers' room. Even so, I was more than a little surprised to find Brittany in the room that day. She also had a difficult workout as a member of the women's track team and needed to soak her sore muscles, just like I needed to soak mine.

The moment I saw Brittany my heart started to race. I started to turn around and walk out, but I knew I couldn't. Ice baths were a crucial part of my training routine. With the Olympic trials just around the corner, I could not afford to skip them.

"Hi, Lopez," she said. "How was your workout today?"

I could hardly hear her with my heart beating so loud in my ears. "Okay, how was yours?"

"Brutal, otherwise I wouldn't be in here."

"Same here," I said. "Have you been in there long?"

"Just climbed in," she said.

"Good," I said. I grabbed a towel and wrapped it around my head to keep me warm. I climbed into a tub on the opposite side of the room from her. Running track all through high school and college, I often found myself in the trainers' room with members of the opposite sex. Even though you soak in the ice tub fully clothed, I always keep a distance between myself and the girls in the room.

"Good?" Brittany asked with a laugh. "What does that mean?"

"Well, I just meant, that will give us time to talk."

"Oh," she said with a funny little tone. "Is there something we need to talk about?" I did not know it at the time, but Baby Mac and Kenny G had already spilled the beans about me wanting to ask her out.

"Well, there's, uh, new African restaurant in town." I paused.

"Yes," she said.

"So I was wondering, if you don't have anything else going on, if you would like to go there with me on Saturday after practice, to, you know, eat something, er, lunch."

"You mean, like on a date?" she asked.

"Uh, yeah," I said.

"I would love to," she said with a smile.

"You would?" I said, very excited. "Wow. Great." After that, I never felt the cold of the ice bath. The two of us talked and laughed until my body went numb. I really hate the cold.

We went to the African restaurant on our first date. For our second, we went to a celebration in a community of lost boys and lost girls in Boulder. One of the girls graduated from college, which called for a party, Sudanese style. We danced and ate traditional dishes late into the night. I knew Brittany was something special when she joined right in, even though everything was foreign to her. This was the start of a very long and happy friendship for both of us. Brittany not only kept dating me, but she went on to study Anthropology of Southern Sudanese Culture at Oxford. She also became instrumental in helping me realize my dream of making a difference in Kimotong.

Even though I met Brittany in Colorado Springs, I reminded myself of the real reason I moved there: to prepare for the Olympic trials. I trained alongside the Academy track team and traveled with the team to several meets at which I competed. Traveling with the Air Force Academy was a new experience. The team did not take a commercial jet. Instead we flew in an AC-130 military cargo plane. Instead of comfortable seats, we strapped ourselves into seats that were a step above wooden benches. The roar of the engines echoed through the metal hull that was not insulated at all. Everyone had to wear earplugs to keep from losing our hearing. I thought my first trip with the Academy team would be a good chance to talk to Brittany. Boy, was I ever wrong.

I ran as a pro for the first time at the Adidas Classic in Los Angeles. I did not win, but I ran well enough to reassure me that I'd made the right choice in turning pro. However, the real highlight of the event did not take place on the track. After my event, I headed over toward the locker room to change out of my race clothes and into my warm-ups for my cool-down laps. I have to do the proper cool-down or my muscles will tighten and put me in danger of injury. My agent met me, and the two of us walked along talking about the race I'd just run. All of a sudden, my agent said, "Hey look. There's Michael."

"What?" I said, looking around from side to side.

"It's Michael," he said again. He pointed across the field to a tall, thin man dressed in jeans and a nice shirt.

My jaw hit the ground.

"Let's go say hello," my agent said.

Before I could reply, my agent had already taken several steps toward the man. Worse yet for nervous me, Michael appeared to be on his way over toward us!

"Michael," my agent said, "I would like to introduce you to Lopez Lomong. Lopez," he said turning toward me, "this is Michael Johnson."

I felt like I had just stepped into a dream. Standing in front of me was the man who changed the course of my life eight years earlier without even knowing it. He looked very different live than he did on a small, grainy, car-battery-operated, black-and-white television. I looked up at him. He was much taller than he appeared on television.

"Mr. Johnson," I said, my voice cracking, "it is an honor to meet you."

Michael reached out and shook my hand, "Call me Michael," he said.

"Okay," I said. I could not wipe the goofy grin off my face. To me, this was like meeting royalty. "I watched you run in the 2000 Olympics while I lived in a refugee camp. I am a runner today because of you."

"That's kind of you to say, Lopez," Michael said with a smile. "I know all about your story. I have to tell you, I've followed your career. You're an excellent runner. I'm proud of you and all you've accomplished already. You keep running the way you are now, and you'll be running in the Olympics yourself soon. I know you can do it."

"Thank you," I said. I walked away from the conversation, but I do not think my feet ever touched the ground. *Wow*, I thought to myself, *if Michael believes in me, I know I'm going to reach my goal.*

My first professional win in the 1500 came at a Reebok event in New York. Later, I won the Sun Angel Invitational in Tempe, Arizona. I didn't win my next meet, the Stanford Invitational, but I ran well enough to stay on track for my ultimate goal. At this stage, my goal was not to win but to hit the Olympic standard time of 3:36, which is also known as the A

Standard. Once I hit this time, I would automatically qualify to run in the Olympic trials in Eugene, Oregon, in June.

My next chance to reach the A Standard came at the Carson Invitational in Carson, California. The race did not start out well. I took a nasty fall when I tripped in the first 100 meters of the race. Skin scraped off of my shoulder and calf, leaving me bruised, burned, and bloody. Luckily for me, the recall gun sounded because I fell so early in the race. I ignored the pain and chose not to notice the blood running down my leg. Instead, when the race started a second time, I focused purely on my goal. Whether I won or lost did not matter. All I wanted to do was to look up at the clock at the end of the race and see a time below 3:36 next to my name.

Four laps later, that's exactly what I saw. I'd reached the first leg of my goal. I'd qualified for the Olympic trials. My dream was within my grasp. Now I just needed to make my final kick and grab hold of it.

TWENTY-ONE

Within Sight

T he first injury of my career came two weeks before the Olympic trials. At the end of my workout while running in stride down the backstretch of the Air Force Academy track, something popped in the back of my right leg. I pulled to a stop. When I tried to take another step, pain shot up the back of my leg. My leg would hardly move. I hopped around on my left leg while trying to get the right to work. Coach Hayes ran over to me. "What happened?"

"I don't know. I was working on pacing and my hamstring started acting up." I could feel it pulling down the back of my leg, but at this point in the season I knew we could not afford an injury. I tried to play it down.

He looked concerned and told me to take a few days easy and get it taken care of right away. He knew hamstring injuries were serious. As a coach, he'd seen many runners pull a hammy and the effects. Basically, you can't run with a hamstring pull. The leg tightens up when you exert it, and you are done. Rest is the best treatment, about two months of rest. We had two weeks.

Because of where I trained, I had lots of really good doctors and physical therapists nearby. The trainers and medical staff at the U.S. Olympic training center were amazing. They did an MRI to make sure it was only a hamstring. From there, I went to see a team of physical therapists who specialize in hamstrings. Over the next few days they used ultrasounds, ice baths, and pressure massages to try to get me back on the track. Coach Hayes insisted I consult the trainers at the Air Force Academy as well. They gave me a set of special exercises to do each day to release the tension in my hamstring and improve my mobility.

The therapy regimen loosened up my leg enough that I could run hills. With the trials right around the corner, I had to run to stay in tip-top shape. Running uphill felt fine. Coming downhill was a different story. I could not put weight on my right leg. But I had to keep training. The trials were too close to take any time off. Since I could not run downhill, I ran as hard as I could up the hill, limped back down, then ran up as fast again until I'd run my quota of laps for the day. Afterward I soaked in an ice bath, then let trainers rub down my leg until it felt like they were about to rub my skin completely off. Coach Hayes was concerned about my injury. I tried to keep it to myself. We had worked too hard for this to get in the way now. I just smiled at him and said, "Don't worry, Coach. This is working. I'll be fine by the time the trials start."

"We leave for Eugene next week," Coach Hayes replied. He was worried; I was not.

"Not a problem," I said with a smile. Honestly, I never for a moment thought I would not run in Eugene. God had brought me this far. I was confident He had something bigger in mind than letting an injury stop me just short of my goal. For me, making the Olympic team transcended sport. Running for the United States on sports' biggest stage would give me a larger platform on which to raise awareness for Sudan and to make a difference for the people there. I also saw this as my chance to give something back to the country that took me in and made me a citizen when I had no home. I was too close to let a little thing like a pulled hamstring slow me down.

I knew my hamstring would improve once we went to Eugene for the trials because a secret weapon waited for us there. Phil Wharton and his dad, Jim, are the best of the best when it comes to musculoskeletal therapy. They know how to fix athletes quickly. I called Phil right after my injury. "Let's meet in Eugene," he told me.

When I arrived there, he'd rented a house where I went for daily therapy. Lots of athletes use the Whartons, not just me. Like I said, they are the best of the best.

Coach Hayes went with me for my therapy session. The environment at Olympic Trials is exhilarating. It is also heavy with tension and expectation. Coach paced around the room, fidgeting, nervous. I stayed calm, and Phil Wharton was excited but focused. The three of us made quite a team. Every day Dr. Wharton worked over my hamstring with a combination of massage and ice. He also put me on a special diet. During the massage sessions he told me over and over, "Don't worry about your leg. Focus on running. You already have an A-standard time, so you aren't chasing anything you haven't already reached. Just go out there and compete—and beat people!" Dr. Wharton was the perfect buffer between me and the nervous intensity of Trials. He took my mind off the fear of the name *Olympic trials*. "It's just a race, Lopez," he told me over and over. "It's just another race." After spending time with him, I was ready to go out and make the United States Olympic team.

The trials kicked off, but my event, the 1500 meters, was still a few days away. Running felt better every day. I decided I needed to test my leg prior to my first 1500 heat. I had entered both the 800 and the 1500 before the trials started. I planned to choose one or the other prior to the actual start of competition and focus solely on that race. I went to Coach Hayes and said, "I'm going to run the 800 just to test my leg speed." Even though I had not run the 800 all season, I ran it throughout college. I liked the race a lot.

He looked at me like I was crazy. "The 1500 is your best shot at making the Olympic team."

"Yes, I know," I said.

"Then why would you choose to do the 800 instead?"

"I'm not. I think I should run the first round of the 800 just to give my leg a little workout before the 1500 starts in a few days."

Now Coach Hayes knew I'd lost my mind. "I don't think that's a good idea. We need to take it easy the next couple of days, then push hard when your race actually starts."

"I won't do anything crazy. I need to stretch out my leg and get ready for my real race. Come on, we're just talking about one heat. No more."

"Okay, but just the one heat," Coach Hayes said.

"Yep, one 800. That's all."

I meant what I said until I actually won my heat. "One more round," I told Coach Hayes. He liked this even less than he liked the idea of me running the first heat. Finally, after much back and forth, he relented. "One more round and no more," he insisted.

"Sure. No problem," I said. I then went out and won that race as well. Now I was in the finals. If I finished in the top three in finals, I would qualify for the Olympics in the 800. I never planned on running in this event. I only ran to get ready for my real race. But now, with the finals and a spot on the Olympic team right in front of me, I could not walk away. I had to go for it.

Coach Hayes came to me. "Lopez, you look awesome out there. However, we cannot jeopardize your chances in the 1500 by letting you run the 800 final. You need to decide which event you really want to run. You've run a lot of good 800s, but the 1500 is your best chance to not only make the Olympic team, but to do something once you get to Beijing."

"I understand," I said, "but I think I can still do both."

Coach Hayes closed his eyes and rubbed his head. "I was afraid you would say that. Look, I have never doubted your ability but I don't want your choices to affect your chances of making the team. The fans love you and want to see you run the 800 final, but we have to think about you here. The best thing to do, the smart thing, is to stop now. Take the next couple of days to rest so you peak in the 1500." The 1500 started the day after the 800 final. Coach was right. No runner in his right mind would do what I was doing.

"I understand," I said.

"So what do you want to do?"

"I have to run in the finals," I said. I knew he was right, but I also knew I would always wonder if I had what it took to make the team in the 800, especially if I did not make it in the 1500.

Coach shook his head but knew I had made up my mind. "This is crazy! To go all the way to the finals in the 1500 will mean running six races in seven days. I know you are one of the most talented athletes out there, but bad choices can compromise that. If that's what you want to do, I know you are capable, but be smart."

"I have to try." I walked away very unsure of myself. What would I do if Coach was right? Had I blown my best chance to make the team by running 800s? I went to see Dr. Wharton for our therapy session. He calmed me down. "Use your head," he told me. "Listen to your body. Don't go beyond what it tells you it can do." I needed him to go talk to Coach Hayes. For a coach, the hardest thing is to watch their athletes go to the track and know they no longer have any control. All of the preparation in the world cannot alleviate the anxiety the coach feels. We faced other obstacles now, but we had planned long and hard for this race. The whole year of training climaxed at this point. I was ready.

I felt great the morning of the 800 final. I did all my warm-ups. My hamstring felt great. As I jogged around the track, other coaches and runners looked at me like I was nuts. I figured this was just one more step toward getting ready for my real event the next day. If I qualified for the Olympics in the 800, great. If not, I would do it in the 1500.

I lined up in lane seven for the start of the 800 meter final. The line has a staggered start, which means those in the outside lines appear to have a head start on the people in the inside. That head start disappears after the first turn. The farther outside you are, the farther you have to run. The stagger makes sure everyone runs the same distance. Lane seven put me in the next to the farthest outside lane.

The gun sounded and I took off. We rounded the first turn and passed the line which tells the runners they can move out of their lanes and toward the inside lane of the track. I pushed hard out of that turn and dove toward the middle. However, other runners bunched up inside, so I stayed just off their outside shoulders in fourth position. I sprinted down the backstretch. Halfway down I pulled into third position. By the time we rounded the second curve and came up the home straightaway, I moved up from third and into second. I don't always like to move up so fast, but I thought it the best strategy for the pace of this race.

We headed into the first curve of the second and final lap. My leg felt strong. *I can do this!* I told myself. I stayed in second all the way through the curve and down most of the backstretch. By this point, I was not thinking about 1500 meters or anything else. I could see my Olympic dream right in front of me, and I wanted to grab it no matter what the cost.

All of a sudden, a runner darted around me. By the time I realized what had happened, he had passed the leader into first place. Other runners started passing me as well until I found myself in fifth place. *Not a problem*, I told myself. I'd outkick them in the final one hundred meters. I dug deep and kicked it into another gear. My feet tore at the track. The first and second place runners were too far ahead to catch, but that did not matter. I just needed to finish in third place to punch my ticket to Beijing.

Push! I screamed at myself. My feet were flying. I pulled into a tie with two other runners for third place The tape was just ahead. I started to lean in, but something held me back. Someone behind me had grabbed hold of my jersey. As I tried to pull free, the guy on the inside lane dove toward the finish line. He tumbled over the line just ahead of me. Officially I came in fifth, less than a tenth of a second out of third place. I came within a jersey tug of making the Olympic team.

After the race, I stood shocked that my Olympic dream had been stolen by a pull of my jersey. I shook, trying to catch my breath and realizing that I had failed to make the Olympic Team. I had tasted it. That is the nature of Track and Field. Not everything goes according to plan.

"No problem," I said to myself. "These things happen." I meant what I said. Once the race was over, my mind could focus on the bigger picture. I ran the 800 as a warm-up for the 1500 and I'd nearly made the Olympic team! My leg was strong. Warm-ups were over. I was ready to go out and give it my all in the 1500. If I ran my race the way I knew I could, I would be on my way to Beijing.

TWENTY-TWO

"Thank You, America!"

T he second injury of my career came ten minutes before the biggest race of my life. I never saw it coming.

Over the previous three days I sailed through the first two rounds of the 1,500 meter Olympic trials even after running three 800 meter races in the days leading up to the first round. My body felt strong. My pulled hamstring felt so good when I ran that I almost forgot I'd injured it. From time to time it would tighten up, but Dr. Wharton always made me good as new. Even Coach Hayes had calmed down a little after watching me run in the semifinal race. My performance finally convinced him that running the 800 meter final did not blow my chance to make the Olympic team in the 1500. We were one heat away. He actually appeared relaxed.

The day of the finals, I was out in the infield grass stretching from side to side when the first call for the 1500 came. I made my way toward the reporting area by doing long strides to finish my stretching. If not for my leg injury, I might have sat down to stretch, but I didn't want to take a chance on my hamstring tightening up. Once I finished my long strides, I planned to have Dr. Wharton do a quick rubdown right before the race to make sure the hamstring was good and loose. I went through the same routine before every race. Now that I was in the final, I saw no point in changing anything.

I took my first couple of long strides. My legs felt great. Then I took my third. My right foot came down on what appeared to be a normal patch of grass. I never saw the small hole into which my foot dropped. I came down on it awkwardly, twisting my ankle on the same leg that had the bad hamstring. Pain shot up my leg. I tried to jog it out, but I couldn't put any weight on my right foot.

"Second call, 1500 meter men's final," the track announcer said. I saw Coach Hayes on the opposite side of the track, but I avoided him. If he saw me limping, he might shatter his cell phone on the ground.

I headed straight to Dr. Wharton. "I have a problem."

"What happened? Is it your hamstring?" he asked.

"No. My hammy feels great, but I twisted my ankle in a hole while doing strides." I spoke very softly so no one else could hear. The race was about to start, and I could hardly walk. I didn't want anyone else to know.

"Oh no. Are you serious? Here, lay down. Let me see what I can do." He grabbed my foot and made a couple of adjustments.

"Third call, 1500 meter men's final."

Coach Hayes walked over to me. He had a puzzled look on his face. "What are you doing, Lopez? Time to report for the race. Why are you laying down now?"

"He twisted his ankle," Dr. Wharton said.

Coach Hayes hid the anxiety. He could not let the injury get to my head. We both knew Dr. Phil was the best at what he did. "Keep focused on the race plan, Lopez. Remember all of the different plans we discussed. You know when to make your move." It was almost that point where he turned me loose. He looked concerned about my ankle but kept me focused on the race plan.

"I'm fine now, Coach," I said. I stood up. The ankle still did not feel right, but I had to go report for the race. They weren't going to delay the finals until my ankle healed.

I grabbed my backpack and my uniform and started over toward the track. As I walked I prayed, *God, I know You gave me this dream for something bigger than myself. You've done too many impossible things in my life so far for me to believe that You want my dream to end like this.*

I took another step. The pain in my ankle disappeared. I took another couple of steps. My ankle felt like I'd never run a race in my life, much less five in the past six days. I ran a couple of strides.

Coach Hayes looked calmly at me. "Go run the race we planned" he said.

"Yep. See you at the finish line."

I handed Coach Hayes my backpack and went over to the reporting station. As I walked up, I heard a couple of coaches talking. "Yeah, Lopez is injured," one said.

"What the heck was he thinking running all those races? He blew his chances," said another.

"Excuse me," I said as I squeezed past them to the reporting desk. They looked at me like they'd seen a ghost. Their shock quickly turned to relief. With me hurt, their guys had an easier path to Beijing. I gave them a slight smile. I knew something they didn't know.

After reporting, I took my place on the start line. Pure joy washed over me. *This is the moment I've been dreaming about for eight years. Kakuma to Tully to Norfolk, Flagstaff to Colorado Springs, and now here, Eugene, Oregon. This is the place. My dream is about to come true!*

"Go, Lopez!" someone yelled from the crowd. I smiled and looked up in the stands. There was Melissa, my friend who brought me photographs of my mother. She wore a red shirt that said, "Run fast, Lopepe," in Swahili. Brittany sat near her. I thought about all the laps the two of us had run together in Colorado Springs getting ready for today. She smiled a huge smile at me. Oh what a wonderful moment this was. I was not running from bullets or away from hunger. No, this was the ultimate moment of running for pure joy.

"Runners, to your marks . . . Get set . . ." The gun sounded. I took off. This was the moment about which I'd dreamed for so long. I planned to enjoy it.

The first two laps went according to my game plan. Stay alert on the first lap, close to the front, eyes all around for anyone who trips, conserve energy for the end. Get in position on lap two. I ran my race. Toward the end of the second lap, I moved to within striking distance of the leaders, while remaining just far enough outside to keep from getting boxed in. The pace picked up on the third lap. I moved closer to the front, ready to strike. The hamstring felt great, no pain in my ankle. God performed a miracle on my leg; there is no other explanation.

We rounded the turn and headed up the straightaway for the bell lap, the final four hundred meters that stood between twelve runners and the United States Olympic Team. Up ahead I saw my cheering section in the stands. All of them stood, screaming my name. I moved up to third position, right where I needed to be.

All of a sudden, I felt a push on my back. I looked to my side. Someone had pushed the guy running next to me, and he fell into me. Everyone in the front pack stumbled and looked ready to fall. My feet flew awkwardly. I struggled to keep my balance while trying to avoid the runners stumbling around me. All of us were on the verge of hitting the ground. *Lopez, it's good. Just run*, I heard God say to me. My feet came back under me. No one fell. The bell sounded. Time to grab the dream.

Lap four of the 1500 is the "God, help me" lap. He already had. I took off around the first turn. I was right where I wanted to be to start my kick at the 300 meter mark. My eyes were open, but I felt like I was running in a dream. *For You, God, and the kids I left behind*, I prayed as I ran. Eight years earlier I wrote an essay as a prayer to God. Now I ran my prayer.

Three hundred meters to go. I started my kick. This was my

opportunity to make my dream a reality. This was the moment about which I'd talked to anyone who would listen since I landed in America. I moved toward the front. I was close enough that I thought I would not just qualify for the Olympic team; I had a chance to win this race.

Two hundred meters to go. The final curve. I pushed my body harder than I had in any race in my life. I dug down for every last reserve of strength within me. Everyone was in their kick. "Lopepe, run fast!" I heard from the stands. With 150 meters to go, in the middle of the curve, running as hard as I could, my hamstring tightened with a yank. Pain shot up my leg and covered my body. "Not now. Not this. Oh God, hear my prayers."

I fell back. Runners passed me. I could not run full speed. More runners passed me, taking my Olympics with them.

I ran out of the curve and onto the final straightaway. Coach Hayes always told me races are won and lost in the final one hundred meters. I pushed, but my body did not respond. My leg hurt and my body wanted to give in to the pain.

Ninety meters to go. Eighty-nine. Eighty-eight. I fell farther behind.

Then something remarkable happened, something I cannot explain. At the eighty-seven-meter mark, a burst of energy came over me and overwhelmed the pain in my leg. My feet flew. I passed one runner, then another. The crowd jumped to their feet, screaming, but I didn't hear anything except the beating of my heart and my feet on the track. Up ahead I saw the first guy cross the tape, winning the race. I did not need to win to make the team. My goal was the top three. A second runner crossed the line. Two spots were taken. The finish line was right in front of me. With one final burst of speed, I passed the last runner as I crossed the line in third place.

I fell to the ground, overjoyed. Up above, my friends chanted my name. I made the sign of the cross. "Thank You, God. Thank You, thank You, thank You. You did this, not me!" I may have run the race, but He was the One who healed my hamstring and my ankle and the One who gave me the power to make that final push. I got up and ran over to the guys who finished first and second. All three of us wore wide smiles. This was an unbelievable moment. "Congratulations," I told them.

"You, too, Lopez. We're going to Beijing!"

Later, the three of us made our way to the podium for the victory ceremony. Along the way I signed one autograph after another. People shook my hand. Others patted me on the back. "Congratulations, Lopez! Great race." At the podium I was asked if I wanted to say anything. "Thank you, America," I said. "Thank you." That pretty much summed up everything in my heart.

Here I was, a former lost boy. Not only did America open up and give me a home, but now I had the privilege of representing her on a world stage. Like Michael Johnson, I would soon run with the letters *USA* across my chest. I could not help but wonder if there would be another boy out there without hope who would see me run. Perhaps he would see me and know his dreams could come true.

I left the podium and made my way through the crowd. More people crowded in for autographs. I signed as many as I could. Then I looked over and saw a small boy. He could not get through the crowd to get close to me. He reminded me of me many years before when the strong boys pushed me out of the way on Tuesdays at the garbage dump in Kakuma. Our eyes met. "Can I have your shoes?" he shouted.

"Sure, kid," I replied. I pulled my shoes off, signed the sides with a pen, and tossed them to him. His father broke out in tears. "Enjoy," I said.

"Thank you!" the boy yelled back.

I walked on through the crowd, barefoot. Somehow, it only seemed right to walk away from the biggest race of my life without shoes. After all, that's how I learned to run. Melissa ran over to greet me. Her parents were with her. All of them cried. Brittany found me in the crowd. We hugged. "You did it," she said.

I smiled. I could hardly talk. The dream had come true.

After all the chaos died down, I went over to the medical tent for the post-race drug test. Afterward, Dr. Wharton took me, Brittany, Coach Hayes, and our friends out in a limo to celebrate. We drove around Eugene celebrating. One of the therapists shouted *"Nihao,* Beijing." I don't know why he did, but before long all of us were shouting it, even Coach Hayes.

"How's the ankle feel?" he asked.

I had to stop and think for a moment. I hadn't thought about the ankle since the gun sounded for the start of the race. "Perfect," I said.

"Unbelievable," he replied.

I smiled. "Yes it is," I said. "Unbelievable" pretty much described my journey from Sudan to Kakuma to the black-and-white, car-battery-powered television to America and now this. Unbelievable and impossible, except for the God who makes all things possible.

TWENTY-THREE

The Highest Honor

W here's Lopez? I want to meet Lopez."

I heard my name, but I could not believe the speaker was looking for me. For eight years I had dreamed of running for the United States in the Olympic Games, but this went beyond anything I could have ever imagined. The president of the United States was now looking for me.

"Over here, sir," one of the coaches said.

President Bush smiled and headed over toward me. He had just delivered a speech to the entire U.S. delegation, which consists of every athlete and coach for every sport in the Olympic Games, from archery to volleyball. All of us were seated in a large gymnasium prior to the Olympic opening ceremonies. In his speech, the president tapped into his old cheerleader self. "Get out there and kick some butt!" he told us. After his speech, he went around the room shaking hands. So many famous athletes I admired were there: Duke's "Coach K," Mike Krzyzewski, Kobe Bryant, Lebron James, Carmelo Anthony, and Dwayne Wade of the

Dream Team. Michael Phelps, who went on to win eight gold medals, was also there.

Yet out of all these incredible and famous athletes, the president wanted to see me. Me! A nobody, a lost boy! For eight years I dreamed of running in the Olympics, but I never dreamed this.

"Mr. President, I would like to introduce you to our flag bearer, Lopez Lomong," the head of the U.S. Olympic Team said. The flag bearer leads the team into the stadium. It is one of the highest honors any Olympic athlete can receive. Unlike medals that are won in competition, the flag bearer is elected by his teammates. Out of the 596 athletes representing the United States in these games, only one can lead the team into the stadium carrying the flag, and that one was me.

President Bush shook my hand. "Lopez, I've heard a lot about you. I just wanted to let you know how excited and happy I am to have you here. Welcome to America. When you go out there and carry that flag tonight, enjoy the moment. It is your flag."

"Thank you, sir," I said. I could not believe I was shaking hands with the president. My mind raced back to watching him in New York the day after the 9-11 attacks. He inspired me as he stood atop a pile of rubble with the rescue workers, a bullhorn in his hand. I had only been in America a few months at the time. That war that had followed me here left me shocked and shaken. Yet President Bush's confidence calmed my fear and let me know that we as a nation would rise above the darkness of that day.

"Let me introduce you to my wife, Laura," the president said. "And this is my mom and dad." I shook each hand in a state of total unbelief. Who gets to meet one president and first lady, much less two? No one else got to talk much to the president because he spent so much of his time with me. Eventually he moved on to greet other athletes. I lost sight of him. I assumed he'd left to go to his seat in the Olympic Stadium.

Everyone in the U.S. delegation, all of the nearly six hundred of us, stood around talking and laughing. We wore the same uniform: white slacks, blue blazers, and white caps. The guys wore ties; the girls did not. I thought back to Coach Paccia bribing me to run cross-country with a Tully High School jacket with my name on it. I could not wait for him to see me now as he watched the opening ceremonies on television back home.

A U.S. Olympic Committee official came over and took me by the arm. "Come with me," he said.

I assumed I needed to go somewhere for instructions on how I was to carry the flag properly. Instead, he took me into a room off to one side. I walked in, and there was the president. "Lopez," he said when he saw me, "come on in here. There's something I forgot to tell you."

I could not imagine what the president needed to tell *me*.

"Yes, sir," I said.

He put his hand on my shoulder. "Lopez, son, when you go out there tonight carrying our flag, don't let it touch the ground, buddy."

"No, sir, I promise you I won't."

"All right. Go get 'em," President Bush said with a laugh. Then he patted me on the back.

"Thank you, Mr. President," I said. I went back to the team, but I do not think my feet touched the ground. No matter what happened from this point forward, these Olympic Games had already exceeded my wildest expectations.

The idea of my becoming flag bearer first arose when one of my friends, a discus thrower named Casey, came up to me in San Jose prior to the team flying to China. "I'm going to nominate you to be the flag bearer," he said to me.

"What are you talking about?" I asked.

"One person carries the flag in for the entire United States delegation in the opening ceremonies. I've talked to some of the other guys, and we think you should be the one to do it."

I thought about that conversation all the way across the Pacific on our flight to Beijing. The more I thought about the possibility of carrying the flag, the more excited I got. I doubted it would happen, but if I've learned anything in my life, it is to never doubt the impossible. The very idea that I could go from a lost boy in a refugee camp to United States Olympian sounded pretty impossible, but here I was. And I was not just on the Olympic team. I was on the team in the Games held in Beijing. I had been here once before during my trip from Nairobi to New York. That trip had also been a dream come true. Now God granted me an even larger dream. After the way He took care of both my hamstring and ankle injuries during the Olympic trials, I knew anything was possible.

After training one afternoon, all the track-and-field athletes met together to elect a track-and-field team captain and to select our nominee for flag bearer. When it comes to the flag bearer, every sport nominates one athlete, which means basketball nominates one, swimming and diving one, gymnastics one, and so on. All the team captains then meet together to elect one person out of all the team nominees as the flag bearer.

The guy running the meeting announced, "If you want to nominate someone, write down the name and turn in your paper up front." After all the paper nominations had been turned in, the coach for all track-and-field read the names of everyone nominated. "If you hear your name, come up to the front." The scene reminded me of sitting in church in Kakuma waiting for my name to be called for a ticket to America. Like then, my name was called. "Lopez Lomong," the coach said. Unlike that day in Kakuma, I did not leap to my feet like I'd been handed a gold medal. I calmly got out of my chair and walked to the front of the room. After the last nominee came forward, the team voted. But the vote took an unexpected turn. One after another, the other nominees said, "I support Lopez," and sat down. Finally, I was the only one left standing.

This was only the first step in the election process. Next, all the team captains met together to vote on the nominees from each team.

Usually this process goes through several ballots. Not in 2008. The captains elected me on the second ballot. One guy from another sport had even said, "If the track team had not nominated Lopez, I was going to do it myself."

When I was first chosen flag bearer, reporters assumed the U.S. team wanted to make a political statement. Around the time of the Olympic trials, I joined a group of athletes called Team Darfur. Created by Joey Cheek, who competed in the 2006 Winter Olympics as a speed skater, Team Darfur spoke out to raise awareness of the genocide occurring in the Darfur region of Sudan. There, the Sudanese government in Khartoum committed the same kind of atrocities they committed in my home region of South Sudan during the civil war that lasted twenty years. In the south, the Muslim government of the north destroyed homes and villages of people who are predominantly animists and Christians. Darfur is a Muslim region. In fact, soldiers from Darfur fought against my people in the south. After fighting in the south ended, the genocide in Darfur began. Arab Sudanese began exterminating African Sudanese. Even though they shared the same religion, the government in Khartoum attacked and nearly wiped out the African Sudanese in the area.

I spoke out against the genocide right after I qualified for the Olympic team. That is why my selection as flag bearer appeared to be a political act. The Chinese government financially supported the Sudanese government in spite of the atrocities. Groups from around the world pressed the Chinese to do something to stop the genocide, but China ignored them. They didn't even let Joey Cheek attend the Olympics because they did not want him to speak out about Darfur. At the last minute they revoked his visa. I thought that was a huge mistake on China's part, and I still do.

But the U.S. team did not give me this high honor because they wanted to make a statement about Darfur. Right after word got out of my selection, a reporter asked me if my election had political implications. I did not take his bait. "I don't have words for how happy I am," I said. "I'm so proud to be an American and raise that flag proudly."

The biggest questions came the morning of my news conference. It was one of many news conferences the U.S. Olympic Committee organized that day. The U.S. basketball team, the Dream Team, was scheduled to talk to the press right after me.

When I went into the conference room, I think reporters expected me to say something about Darfur and China's role in it. As important as that topic may be, I knew what I had to do. I sat down and proceeded to tell my story. I talked about the day I was taken from my church and of being held in the rebel prison camp. I told the story of my escape through the wilderness with my three angels and of my years in Kakuma. I shared the story of watching Michael Johnson run in the 2000 Olympics and the dream he gave me. Then I explained how America opened its arms to me and gave me this great opportunity. "I am so thankful for this privilege of getting to put on this jersey and represent my country," I said.

At first I felt nervous. But as I shared my story a peace came over me. I knew this moment was why God put me in this position. This wasn't just my story. He gave me this chance to speak up for all the lost boys and girls and for everyone who suffers from the unjustness of war.

"I hope I'm here to inspire other kids who are out there watching these Olympics, as I did watching the Sydney Olympics. I hope . . . all the countries and all the nations are there watching and they will learn from where I came from," I said.

Once the press was finished with me, I walked out in the hallway. I needed to get back to training for my event. With all the media buzz surrounding me as the flag bearer, I almost forgot I actually had a race to run in a few days. The president of the USOC walked out with me. "Good job, Lopez. You were great in there," he said.

"Thank you. I spoke from my heart," I said. "If you are through with me, I need to go train."

"Sure. I understand. I need to get back in there for the next press conference. See you at the opening ceremonies."

I turned to leave when a girl went up to the USOC president and whispered something in his ear.

"Really?" he said to the girl. "Okay. We can do that." Then, turning to me, he said, "Lopez, I need you to do one more thing before you go. Coach K would like for you to say a few words to the basketball team."

My jaw hit the floor. "The Dream Team?"

He laughed. "Yes, the Dream Team. Follow Susan here and she'll take you to them."

The next thing I knew, I was next to Coach Mike Krzyzewski, the legendary Duke University basketball coach. Coach Jim Boeheim from Syracuse stood off to one side. Coach K put his hand on my shoulder. "We watched your news conference."

"You did?" I could not believe this.

"We sure did. Listen, I need you to do me a favor. I want you to tell your story to my team exactly like you told it in that news conference. Tell these guys what it means to be an American and what it means to wear that jersey. I don't think any of us understand it quite like you do."

"Are you serious? Me?"

"Yes, I am, Lopez," Coach K said.

I walked into the green room and into the presence of athletic royalty. The room was filled with guys I'd not only watched on television, but I wore their jerseys out on the driveway shooting baskets at home in Tully, New York. Kobe Bryant sat on one side of the room near Lebron James. Carmelo Anthony, who went to college in Syracuse, sat close to the front. The greatest basketball players in the world filled this room, and their coach wanted me to talk to them.

My knees nearly knocked and my voice cracked a little when I started talking. But I did exactly what Coach asked me to do. I told my story. Outside, media people walked the hall, looking for the Dream Team, who was now late for their news conference. The coaches did not care.

"We will be out once Lopez is finished," an assistant told a USOC media representative who knocked on the door. Inside the room, every eye was locked onto me. All these guys sat in complete silence as I spoke. They soaked in every word.

After I finished speaking, Coach K got up. "Now you guys know what this is all about. You are ambassadors for our great country. Now go out there and get it done." The team broke out in huge applause. Afterward I posed for photographs with the team. One player after another shook my hand and told me how much they appreciated what I said. I walked out of the room with a standing invitation to come hang out with the team whenever I wanted. More than that, I knew many of these guys were already involved in helping people in need both in the United States and around the world. It felt good to share my passion to make a difference in the lives of others.

I thought I was nervous when I spoke to the Dream Team. I was *really* nervous when it came time to put on the strap for the flag and walk out into Beijing's Olympic Stadium, also known as the Bird's Nest. The flag was huge, and the wind whipped down the tunnel where I waited for the signal to start walking. *"Don't let that flag touch the ground, buddy,"* the president had told me. At the time I did not think that would be hard. With the wind blowing, I was not so sure. And I knew he was watching me from his box up above, he and one hundred thousand other people—along with perhaps a billion people on television around the world.

I placed the flagpole firmly in the holder at the bottom of the strap. *Oh God, hear my prayers. Let my cry come to You,* I prayed. This was my moment, the moment God had in mind when He made my Olympic dreams come true. As soon as I stepped on the track, people around the world would hear my story. Once my story got out there, I knew God would also open doors for the bigger dreams I had for my people in

Kimotong. The rest of the United States delegation gathered behind me in the tunnel. A buzz went up from the team. Every face wore a smile. Most of the athletes carried small American flags. All of us were here to celebrate. We were just waiting for the word to go inside the stadium and let the party begin.

I took a deep breath and said another quick prayer. The official in charge of the order of the teams looked up at me. "Okay, it's time," he said. A Chinese girl with a sign that read "United States of America" took her place in front of me. The official pointed down the tunnel. I took off walking.

I stepped out of the tunnel and onto the track that led around the inside of the stadium. A million camera flashes went off at once. The crowd cheered. Peace filled me. I walked down the track, my grip tight on the flagpole. I looked up at the giant Jumbotron television screen. There on the screen I saw President Bush, standing, saluting the flag. They then split the image in half. On one side was the president, his hand over his heart. On the other side was me, Lopez Lomong, the lost boy carrying the flag of his new home. I am no longer a lost boy or an orphan. The flag in my hand is my identity; it is who I am now and who I never was before.

I walked down the track, beaming with pride. God had brought me so far, through war, through eating garbage and running to forget about my empty stomach. No matter what I went through, God was always with me. He had always had this moment planned for me through both the good times and the bad, from the killing fields of Sudan to these Olympic Games and back again.

The trip around the track with the flag was going by too fast. I felt the entire US team pushing me along, carrying me through this moment. Up ahead, a cameraman walked backward. He focused his camera close in on me. Far away, in a living room in Tully, New York, my mom and dad wept with joy.

Farther away still, in a small room in Kenya, my mother and family watched the opening ceremonies on the twenty-inch color television I bought for them on my last trip to Africa. My mother's eyes immediately focused on my left hand. There, on my fingers that gripped the flagpole so tight, was the ring she gave me so I would never forget her. When she saw the ring, she fell to the ground and wept. Through that ring, I told her that I did not make this journey alone. She was right there beside me as well.

A full week passed between the opening ceremonies and my first 1500 meter heat. I needed that time to come down out of the clouds. My mom and dad came before my first race. The entire town of Tully had a huge fund-raiser to send my parents to Beijing. In fact, the day I called my dad to tell him that I'd been elected flag bearer, he and Mom were at the fund-raiser. I thought they were at home. I told him, "I'm going to carry the flag in the opening ceremonies." He turned around and announced it to this huge crowd of people in my hometown. Over the phone I heard the celebration. Everyone shouted and cheered and clapped. After that, the town raised more than enough for my parents to come watch me run in the Olympics.

Jim Paccia, my high school coach who bribed me to run with a Tully High jacket with my name on it, also came to Beijing, as did my best friend from high school cross-country, Tom Carraci. Six years earlier Tom promised he would come to watch me run in the Olympics, and he kept his word. Unfortunately, Brittany had to report to the Air Force Academy the first week of August, which meant she could not come to Beijing. She plans on being there in 2012 and 2016 and 2020. Like I said, Beijing will not be my last Olympics.

My first race came on August 15. I finished fifth, but my time was less than half a second out of first place. My place and time qualified me for the semifinals. That race didn't go quite as well. I approached the semifinals with the same strategy I always use in the 1500 meter. My hamstring still did not feel completely right, but it felt good enough that I was confident I could make the finals. However, through the first two laps it felt worse than it had at any time going back to the day I pulled it in Colorado Springs. I did my best to ignore my leg. *Focus, focus, focus,* I told myself as I rounded the first curve of the third lap. I needed to get into position to make my move in lap four. Going around the curve I felt the hamstring tugging. Curves are harder on this kind of injury than straightaways. *Okay, that's fine,* I reminded myself, *stretch it out on the straightaways then take it a little easier on the curves.*

My strategy worked down the back stretch and into the second curve of the third lap. However, the moment we came out of the curve, everyone broke into their kick. I couldn't believe my eyes. We still had five hundred meters to go. In all my previous races, no one kicked until the three hundred meter mark. When everyone kicked, I tried to keep up. My hamstring said no. I tried to push myself into a higher gear, but my right leg did not respond. I came away with my worst time of the year, a full five seconds slower than my time in the quarterfinals.

I put my hands on my head to catch my breath after I crossed the finish line. The times from my race flashed up on the scoreboard. Right then I knew I could and would do better in my next Olympics. The winning time in my semi-final race was 3:37.04. I ran a 3:36.70 in the quarterfinals. If I had run anything close to my quarterfinal time, not only would I have qualified for the finals, I might have won my semifinal race. Those times told me I can compete at this level. In 2008 I was overjoyed to make the team. Next time, my goal is to bring home a gold medal.

After my cool-down lap and post-race drug test, I left the stadium to find my parents. Mom gave me a huge hug. "I am so proud of you," she said. Dad patted me on the back. He kept shaking his head with a wide grin like he could not believe where he was.

"You ran a good race," he said. "I can't wait to watch you run in London."

Jim Paccia, my high school coach, added, "I have a surprise for you." He then pulled out our old team flag that we made for the cross-country team at Tully High.

I doubled over laughing. "I told you I was going to the Olympics," I said.

"I never doubted you," he said. He then pulled out another surprise. "You know, we won't get to hear the national anthem play for you in the stadium, so I think we need to do something about that." He took out an American flag. I grabbed one side, he took the other. With the flag in front of us, Jim started singing "The Star Spangled Banner." I joined in. Thousands of people filled the plaza around us, but we did not care. Coach and I sang at the top of our lungs. Other Americans in the crowd came over and started singing with us. We finished the last line, and everyone cheered. People chanted, "USA, USA." Then someone recognized me. "Oh my goodness. Lopez is here!" I signed autographs and laughed and talked with fans. I felt like I had just won the gold, silver, and bronze medals combined. Mom and Dad soaked it all in. It was a moment I will never forget.

TWENTY-FOUR

Passing the Dream
to My Brothers

A couple of months after returning home from Beijing, I received autographed copies of the photographs I'd taken with the President and Mrs. Bush. Along with the photographs came an invitation to join my fellow U.S. Olympians at the White House. As much as I wanted to go, I had to decline. Just like after winning the 2007 NCAA Championship, I had another, more pressing opportunity. I guess it is only fitting that my new opportunity grew directly out of the first.

The night HBO aired the *Real Sports* profile of my life in late 2007, a track coach in Virginia and his wife happened to tune in. By the time the story ended, Winston and Beth Brown knew they had to do something about what they had just seen. Winston teaches and coaches cross-country and track at Fork Union Military Academy in Virginia. Although it sounds like a boot camp, it is not. The school is a Christian academy for boys in grades six through twelve. Coach Brown made several phone calls and held many meetings before contacting me. I met him for the first time at the Olympic trials. He introduced himself to me and then dropped a bomb: "I want to help you bring your brothers to America."

I could not believe my ears. Since the day I left Peter and Alex a year earlier, I had prayed for a way to bring them to America to get an education, but I did not even know where to start. Even though they attended school in Kenya, their school cannot prepare them for college. And a college degree is my goal for my little brothers.

"You're kidding me," I said to Winston. "That is very generous of you."

"You story touched us," he said. "I figured this is one small thing we can do to make a difference."

"This is not small," I said to him. "A good education means everything."

Winston went on to tell me about Fork Union Academy. He told me how it is a Christian school that focuses on preparing students to go to college. His words were music to my ears. "The school is a boarding school, but my wife and I want your brothers to live with us, if that's okay with you. We want to give them the experience of a family like what you had with your American mom and dad."

With those words, this man in Virginia and his wife went from being strangers to family. By the time I returned from Beijing, Winston had completed all the paperwork needed to start the immigration process for my brothers. However, I could not just jump on an airplane and go get Peter and Alex. Back when I came, all I had to do was write one essay. That was easy. The real work was done before I ever heard about the chance to come to America by people at Catholic Charities whose names I do not know. Now that I was on the other side, I had a new appreciation for all they did for me. With Peter and Alex, I had to fill out mountains of papers from three different countries. The process took months, even though Winston Brown had already completed a large portion of it for me.

During this time I also tried to bring my sister, Susan, to the States. However, I faced two insurmountable problems. First, Fort Union

Academy is an all-boys' school. I could not find another school will-ing to accept my sister. Without a school in place, I could not apply for a student visa for her. On top of that, Susan was afraid of leaving the family and the familiar surroundings of Kimotong. She is the only girl in the family. The thought of leaving our mother filled her with dread. She just could not do it. No matter what I said, her mind was made up. Rather than argue with her, I focused my efforts on Peter and Alex. I still pray that someday I can bring Susan to the United States.

By the time the invitation to the White House came, I had moved far enough along in the process of bringing my brothers to America that I could finally go to Sudan for the next round of paperwork. I traveled with my mother and brothers to the city of Juba, Sudan. My mother, brothers, and I went to the government offices to try to get my brothers' passports. In most African countries, children are not born in hospitals. As a result, we do not have birth certificates. Without birth certificates, it is difficult to get a passport.

We took three witnesses from our village who basically had to tell the government, "Yes, I know these boys. They were born in Kimotong and this is their mother." However, the clerk almost did not sign off on the paperwork. He looked at me, the English-speaking American, my two brothers who spoke Swahili almost exclusively after going to school in Kenya, and my Buya-speaking mother, and asked with a suspicious tone, "How are you people connected?" Thankfully, he believed me when I told him this was my mother and brothers and that I was going to take my brothers to America. Either he believed me or he did not care enough to try to stop me. Either way, we got our passports.

Once I had my brothers' passports, we traveled south to the United States embassy in Nairobi, Kenya. On the way I told my mother once again, "I am taking Peter and Alex back to America with me." The first time I told her months earlier, she said something like, "Good. These boys are driving me crazy." Back then she did not think I was serious. Now she knew I was.

"Why do you have to take them away to America? Why don't you stay here with them?" My mother never quite understood why I had not moved back to Africa once she found me alive.

"Mother, I've told you. America is my home now. I am a United States citizen. I go to college there. I am a professional athlete."

"Why do you want to take Peter and Alex?"

"So they can get a college education, just like me."

We had this same conversation over and over all the way from Juba to her house in Juja, Kenya. I never convinced her, but she did not stand in my way. "Okay, you can take them. But you have to bring them back home to me after they get their education," she said. She had given her approval, but deep down, she hoped they would stay with her.

My mother almost got her wish. For two months I went round and round with the staff at the United States embassy. The embassy grounds are officially United States territory, but all the workers are Kenyan. I have nothing in my heart but gratitude to the Kenyan nation and people for giving me a safe place to live for ten years, but my experience at the embassy nearly took away all the goodwill I had for the place.

Several days each week I made my way from my mother's home in Juja to the embassy in Nairobi. A nine o'clock appointment meant arriving at nine, then sitting and waiting for hours upon hours. The embassy has the look and feel of a post office. When my name was finally called, I had to go to a little window and speak to a Kenyan woman through a phone like something out of a prison movie. She would tell me I had to have another piece of paperwork, or the piece I spent the previous day tracking down had now expired and had to be redone. The new paperwork always meant spending more money. Finally I tossed my Visa card through the slot below the window to the woman and told her, "Here, take everything you need at once. Let's get this over with. I need to get back to America."

Weeks turned into months. When I first flew to Africa, I assumed I could secure their visas in time for them to start school at the beginning of the spring semester. Now we were into February. They had missed more than a month of class and we were no closer to getting home. The stress took its toll. I lost at least twenty pounds and spent thousands of dollars.

Back to the embassy I went. *Oh God, hear my prayer. Let my cry come to You. Please help me get these boys to America.* I arrived at the embassy with my brothers right on time for my nine o'clock appointment. This day, Peter and Alex had to wait outside in the heat. I walked into the waiting area in front of the line of post office windows. *Let me please speak to an American today,* I prayed. I thought if I could just talk to an American, I could make my case and cut through this red tape.

I found a seat and sat down. Nine o'clock, ten o'clock, eleven, twelve, one. I did not know why we had to come so early just to wait. All of our paperwork was in order. The passports were signed. The scholarship papers from the Academy checked out as genuine. Everything was supposed to be in place. All I needed was to have the embassy stamp my brothers' visas in their passports and send us on our way.

"Lomong, window thirteen," the intercom said. I went to the window. The same Kenyan woman with whom I'd dealt too many times sat on the other side. I had already figured out that she looked down on Sudanese people. To her, we are nothing but useless refugees. I could see in her eyes that she did not think we deserved to go to America. She didn't care that I was a United States citizen. In her eyes, I was a lost boy from Kakuma. No one cares about lost boys.

Once again I picked up the phone and made my case. We went back and forth. But today, God answered my prayers. An American walked behind her. He recognized me from the Olympics. "What's the problem?" he asked. I explained my case to him. He picked up my file and read through it. The woman sat very still. She wasn't happy. "Oh sure, we can clear this up quickly. Just give me a little time to get everything signed. Come back tomorrow and we will have you on your way. And if you have any problems, come find me." I thanked him and went out to find my brothers.

The next day I returned to the embassy. Peter and Alex stayed in Juja. I gave them money to get a real haircut. They were also supposed to take a shower and pick out their best clothes for our trip to the United States. I'd already purchased our tickets to leave on a flight that night.

At the embassy I once again found a seat in the large waiting area. A crowd of people waited for their names to be called. Once we hear our name, we go to the window, talk through the phone, then pick up our papers that the worker slides to us through a slot below the glass. I waited all day. My name was never called. The room went from bursting at the seams to empty. I went to the window. Again, I came face-to-face with the same woman. "Can I help you?" she said, hardly even looking up at me.

"I came to pick up my brothers' passports with their visas." I could see their passports lying on the desk behind her.

"They are not ready yet."

"I can see them behind you."

"I cannot give them to you because you have not paid the fee."

"What fee? I've paid all the fees."

"You need to pay another two hundred and thirty dollars."

"Why?" I asked. Anger rose up in me.

"Because they are Sudanese," the woman said with a matter-of-fact tone.

"How horrible are you? God knows what you are doing and you will answer to Him someday. Who is Sudanese? Who is Kenyan? Who is American? We are all people made by God! We are all equal. I want to speak to your manager."

"I am the manager."

"Let me speak to an American."

"I'm sorry. Come back next week."

I was about to go nuts. I had already purchased tickets for a flight that night. Next week was not an option. Right before I completely lost my temper, God intervened. The American who had helped me the day before walked into the office.

"Lopez," he said, "did you get your brothers' passports and visas? Did we get everything worked out for you?"

I glared at the woman. "No," I said. The man looked shocked.

"Oh, here they are," the woman said. She shoved the passports through the window below the glass.

I acted like I did not see them. "This woman said I had to pay another two hundred and thirty dollars because my brothers are Sudanese."

"What?" he said. "What difference does that make?"

"You ask her, sir," I said. I grabbed the passports and walked out.

I went back to my mother's house, expecting to find my brothers clean and shining. Instead, they were outside playing in the dirt, no haircut, no showers, no clean clothes. Obviously they did not have a clue as to what was about to happen to them. I got them cleaned up and ready for our flight. We said a tearful good-bye to our mother at her house and headed for the airport.

The joy I felt walking onto the plane bound for America with my brothers was unlike anything I'd ever experienced. I melted into my seat. All the hard work, all the headaches with the embassy, were worth it to have these two next to me on the plane. I felt more like a proud dad than a brother. I looked at the two of them as they checked out the magazines in their seats' back pockets. As good as I felt about bringing them to America, I knew I wanted to do more. Now I just had to find a way to balance training as a professional athlete, working to make a difference in South Sudan, and, of course, finishing my college degree.

TWENTY-FIVE

The Greatest Moment!

T he biggest moment of my life did not take place in Beijing. Nor was carrying the United States flag in the opening ceremonies my greatest flag-bearing experience. No, my greatest moment when my wildest dreams came true came just over three years after the 2008 Olympics. Nothing compares to it, for not only did it mark my greatest accomplishment thus far in my life, an accomplishment I never imagined possible ten years earlier, it forever changed my future. Now, standing on the other side, I know nothing is impossible. A whole new world of opportunity has been opened to me, opportunities I will pursue the rest of my life. People who grew up in America may not understand what I just wrote. To fully appreciate why December 16, 2011, was the greatest moment of my life, you must go back with me to Kimotong and Kakuma.

My village in Sudan was and is very poor by American standards. No one owns a car. No one has electricity. But worst of all, there is no school in Kimotong. Very few people can read and write because there is no place to learn and no one there to teach them. As I wrote before, parents in

Kimotong who want to give their children an education must send them to Kenya. Only the wealthiest people can afford to do that.

When I was a boy, my father occasionally talked about sending my brothers and sister and me to Kenya for school. He dreamed of giving this gift to us, but he had no way of making the dream come true. Although we were wealthy in terms of our herd of cows, my parents did not have the money to send any of us away to school. Even if they had, I would have received only the most basic education. I might have learned to read and write and do basic math. With luck, I might have graduated from high school, but that is unlikely. By the time I was old enough and big enough to go to high school, the needs of the family farm would have brought me back to Sudan. In Kimotong, you farm by hand, which means you need lots of hands to produce a successful crop.

No, I never would have received the most basic education if I had spent my life in Kimotong. But of course, I did not spend my life there. After the rebels kidnapped me at the age of six, I never thought I would see my home again. If I had been bigger, the rebels would have given me an education. They taught all the bigger boys how to march and how to shoot and how to kill. I was too small for those lessons. They left me behind in the hut where I would either grow big enough to become a soldier, or I would die. They did not care which path I took.

After my escape with my three angels through the wilderness, I arrived in the Kakuma refugee camp poor and hungry. I started school soon after, but it was not the school of which my father dreamed. As I wrote before, because we lacked books, we sang most of our lessons. Most days we sang for two hours or more. I learned history through songs, along with math and English and most every subject. When it came time to write lessons out by hand, I did not have access to paper or pencil. A few boys did, those lucky enough to be sponsored by someone outside the camp. No one ever sponsored me, which meant I wrote my lessons in the dirt with a stick. The teacher came over to me, told me to write an *A*, and I scratched it out in the dust as best I could. If I wrote the letter correctly, the teacher walked on to the boy next to me. If I wrote it incorrectly, the teacher gave me a swat with a switch. "Why did you write it like that?" they barked.

For ten years I did my lessons in the dirt with a stick, and I learned everything that constituted a well-rounded education in Kakuma through song. Never once did I ever think I might one day move on from the camp school and go to college. I might as well have dreamed about flapping my arms and flying to the moon. Given the state of education in Kakuma, the moon was a more realistic dream. Even after ten years of school, I read, wrote, and did math on a first-or second-grade level when I arrived in the United States. I came here, not dreaming of a college education. No, I just hoped to learn enough English to get a job with which I could support myself while sending money back to my friends in Kakuma.

Since you have made it this far in this book, I know you already know everything I just wrote. But I needed to refresh your memory for you to fully grasp what I am about to say.

The greatest moment of my life came on December 16, 2011, when I walked into the Sky Dome on the campus of Northern Arizona University carrying the banner of the W. A. Franke School of Business. It took me a little longer to get here than I had planned. After I left school to turn pro at the end of the fall 2007 semester, I only had three semesters left to graduate. However, I could only attend classes in the track off-season. I took as many classes as I could online, but the pace was still too slow. Finally, in the fall of 2011, I moved back to Flagstaff and took twenty-two hours of classes to finish my degree all at once. That semester was my final academic kick, like the last three hundred meters of a 1,500 meter race. It was hard, but the moment I walked into the Sky Dome carrying my school's banner, I forgot all about the difficulties. This was my victory lap.

I was one of four flag bearers in the commencement ceremony, each of whom represented one of the four colleges within NAU. I carried the banner using the very belt I wore in Beijing. The crowd was much smaller than the Olympic opening ceremony, but for me, the size of the crowd meant far less than the people who were there. On one side of the Sky Dome sat Brittany and her family. They drove down to Flagstaff just to support me. And on the other side of the Sky Dome sat two people who never for a moment doubted this day would come, my mom and dad, Rob and Barbara Rogers.

As soon as I walked through the door of the dome, I heard my parents cheering for me. I turned my head just a little as I walked in, and I spotted them. My mom held up two signs. One said, "Congratulations, Lopez!" The other said, "You did it!" I tried to play it cool, but the sight of those signs made me break out in a smile.

I placed the banner in the flag holder on the stage, then went back to join my seat in the midst of my fellow graduating seniors. Up above, mom pulled out another sign she'd made. I laughed. I glanced around the Sky Dome at all the people. *This cannot be real!* I thought. This had to be a dream. I flashed back to my days of writing my lessons in the dirt in Kakuma. *How did this happen?! Who would have ever thought this possible?!* A wave of pure joy washed over me. The moment the wave hit my feet, I started dancing. No one thought it odd, because several of my fellow graduates were also dancing around. This was the biggest, greatest party I could ever imagine.

Once the speakers took their places on the platform, I had to stop dancing and sit down. The president of the college spoke, then another speaker. I think one of the students may have also talked, but I wasn't paying much attention. I felt like at any moment I would lift up out of my chair and fly around the dome a few times, I was so happy.

Back when my mom first started talking about college to me, I thought she was crazy. I failed as many classes as I passed my first semester at Tully High School. A handful of F's didn't dampen her enthusiasm for school for me, nor did it ever cause her to doubt what I could do. Late at night, as I sat at the computer trying to type out an essay in a language I did not think I would ever master, she would come over to me and tell me, "You can do this, Joseph. You are smart and you are not afraid to work hard. I know you will accomplish anything you set your mind to. Anything is possible for you."

I have to be honest. During my first couple of semesters of high school, my mom believed in my abilities far more than I did. But slowly but surely I started to catch on and catch up. The day I graduated from high school, my mom cried like a baby. Now I looked up at her and Dad in their seats in the Sky Dome. She wasn't crying yet, but I knew it was only a matter of time.

Finally the moment I had been waiting for arrived. The speakers stopped talking. I and my fellow students stood. A little over 2,000 of us slowly made our way to the platform to receive our degrees. I smiled so wide I'm sure my mother in Kenya had to be able to see it. With each name that was called, I moved forward another couple of steps, dancing the whole way. On the outside, I contented myself with a little happy swaying back and forth. On the inside, I was jumping up and down like crazy.

The line moved along. I arrived at the steps leading up onto the platform. Each of us carried a name card, which also listed our degree program. I held out my card, and went up the three stairs. A girl took my card. She handed it over to the announcer. I looked across the stage. The guy in front of me shook hands with the university president. Then I heard these words, "Lopez Lomong, graduating with a bachelor of science in hotel and restaurant management." I knew in my heart at that very moment my mom would break down in tears. And she did.

I walked across the stage. "Congratulations," the president said to me as he handed me a blue folder. "I am very proud of you."

"Thank you," I said as I shook his hand. Winning a gold medal in London will not feel better than the weight of that folder in my hand. I floated on across the stage, shaking hands with the other faculty members. Even though I knew my real degree was not yet in the folder, I instinctively kissed it. Then I held it up toward heaven, just as I hold up my arms after winning a big race. This was bigger than any race I'd ever run. I can run 1,500 meters in a little over three and a half minutes. Winning this race had taken a lifetime spread out over two continents separated by the Atlantic Ocean.

I stepped off the stage and started toward my seat. A hand reached out and grabbed me. The hand belonged to my mentor, Professor Jon Hales. "Congratulations, Lopez. You worked hard for this moment," he said.

"Thank you, sir," I said.

I tried to shake his hand, but he pulled me in and gave me a huge hug. "This is the start of a new chapter in your life. I'm proud of you," he said.

"Thank you for everything you've done for me," I said. Professor Hales pushed me and encouraged me while I was a full-time student at NAU. Once I turned pro, he kept in contact with me. He made sure I did not lose sight of my education goal.

I left Professor Hales and danced back to my seat. "I've made it," I said over and over. "I've made it."

My talk with myself didn't last long. As soon as I returned to my seat, I found myself back in the celebration. Everyone high-fived one another, laughing and celebrating. After the last person had walked across the stage, the announcer said something like, "Congratulations, Class of 2011. You may turn your tassels." Confetti rained down from the ceiling and a loud cheer exploded from the crowd.

I reached up and moved my tassel from one side of my hat to the other. As I did, I let out a yell of jubilation. Afterward, my family and Brittany's family went out to celebrate. It reminded me of the night we all celebrated my making the 2008 Olympic team. This night was better, much, much better.

Even after reading all this you may not understand how graduating from college is, for me, far greater than running in the Olympics or carrying the flag into the opening ceremonies for our national team. After all, I spent time with the president of the United States himself in Beijing. He patted me on the back and sent me off with the words, "Don't let the flag touch the ground, buddy." What can compare to that?

Yet, Beijing represented an accomplishment that culminated in a single moment. I will forever look back on it and smile. I still have a little trouble believing it happened to me. However, walking across the stage at Northern Arizona University and receiving my degree represents both a past accomplishment and the future that now lays wide open to me. My life is now forever changed, as will be the lives of the generations that follow me. More than that, this degree in my hand speaks to the plans I have for my future, and even greater plans God has for me.

Jeremiah 29:11 says, "'For I know the plans I have for you,' says the LORD. 'They are plans for good and not for disaster, to give you a future and a hope.'" These words sound like God wrote them specifically for me. I lived through disaster. I lived through hardship and death. Yet God never left me. He changed me from Lopez the lost boy to Joseph. And just like Joseph in the Bible, He took what was once intended for evil and transformed it into good. Receiving my college degree along with the future that degree represents is the ultimate expression of God turning disaster into a future and a hope, at least so far.

Now that I have finished this race, I want my experience to encourage the other lost boys and girls out there that they, too, have hope of something more. Whether they are in a refugee camp in Kenya, or in the projects of an American inner city, anything is possible for them. If Lopez Lomong can go from a rebel prison camp to college graduate, so can they. The day I graduated from college, I knew beyond a shadow of a doubt that anything is possible. That's not just true for me, but for anyone who is willing to work hard and let nothing stand in the way of reaching their dreams.

I've reached the end of this book, but my story has only really started. I feel like I am standing at the starting line of the biggest race of my life. The gun is about to sound. My opponents surround me, but I am not nervous. No, I am excited. I cannot wait to start the race. I cannot wait to take off, running for joy in a race that will not end until God takes me home.

Still Running for My Life

Over the past few years, I have made many trips back to Kimotong and South Sudan. Every trip left me convinced that the problems the people there face can be resolved. However, doing so will require a team effort. Out of conversations with friends and other athletes, I came up with the idea to start my own foundation. There was only one problem: I did not know anything about starting a charitable foundation. Something like that never stopped me before. I decided I needed to talk to one of my good friends, Tim Lawrence, who has experience with nonprofits. Tim owns a media company in Oregon. Over the years he did several projects for nonprofit groups working in Africa.

Even though Tim had worked with nonprofits, he did not know how to start one. But he saw no reason for that little detail to get in the way. That's why we are such good friends. Neither of us knows the meaning of the word *impossible.* He just had one question for me: "What specifically do you want to do there?"

I'd thought a lot about that question for a very long time. The way I see it, there are four basic needs that must be addressed to improve the lives of the people in South Sudan. First, we need clean water. Today, women spend a large portion of their day walking to the river to fetch water. They carry large buckets of water back to the village on their heads. Even then, the water is not very clean. Waterborne diseases strike regularly all over the world where people do not have access to clean water. But that is not the only danger. My sister was ambushed and raped on her way to the river for water. Something as simple as a well in the middle of the village could have protected my sister. Just thinking about this makes me angry.

Second, I want to open up access to education. I brought my two youngest brothers to America so that they could receive an education. At the time, I had no other good options. My brothers have excelled in school, and not just because I told them they would be on the next plane back to Africa if they screwed up. They have done so well in school because they want to learn. They want an education. Other Sudanese boys and girls are just as eager to learn, but they do not have access to education. I want to change that by building a school in Kimotong. In addition, I want to provide vocational training for women in my village and the surrounding areas. Access to education is limited in the area, but women have it even worse. Education is power, and I want to empower my sister and my mother and the other women of our village and give them a real future.

Education is important, but people cannot learn when they are malnourished. My third priority is to improve nutrition by opening up access to better farming tools and methods. Thousands of years ago, farmers all over the world used a long pole or stick to break up the soil and plant their crops. Across much of Africa they still do. I didn't know you could farm any other way until I came to the United States. Why do we have access to these methods in America, but not in Sudan and other parts of Africa? In Kakuma, my food came in bags from the USA. I used to stare at the American flag on the bag of corn. That food kept me alive. However, one of the best days in Kakuma came when someone gave us seeds so that we could grow our own food. That's what I want to do for my people in South Sudan. I want to help find a way to enable them to feed themselves.

Finally, I have never been able to erase the image of the poor mothers who brought their children to me, asking me to give their children medicine to make them well. I could not do anything to help on that first trip. I came away not only frustrated but angry. The simplest medicines, the most basic of health care, would have saved many of those children. A hospital in Kimotong would be a godsend, but even a small clinic will save lives. I want to start with the latter. Maybe, someday, a hospital will come to the area as well.

When Tim asked me what I wanted to do in South Sudan, all of the above poured out of me. He looked at me for a moment without saying a word. Then he said, "Sounds good to me. Let's get started."

Not long after that, Tim and I found ourselves in a meeting with Stephen Hass of World Vision. A woman named Diane Paddison connected us with World Vision when she and I met at an event where we both spoke. She heard me share my vision for my foundation and for South Sudan, which is why she put me in touch with World Vision. They were already doing many of the things I hoped to accomplish. Partnering with an organization like World Vision made sense to me. It doesn't make much sense to reinvent the wheel when you can join forces with a group that already has a presence in the area.

Even so, I was a little nervous going into the meeting with World Vision. I did not know how they would feel about working with me. I also didn't want my dreams for the area to get swallowed up and forgotten. All of this was new to me. I did not know what to expect. I will never forget what Steven said to me in that meeting. He looked me in the eye and said, "Lopez, you need to understand that we as an organization are committed to any work we start. We plan on keeping a presence in South Sudan as long as we're able to help communities develop themselves. We're going to be there whether you choose to work with us or not."

That's all I needed to hear. "I'm in," I told him.

Out of that meeting emerged 4 South Sudan, a unique partnership between my foundation and World Vision. A portion of the proceeds from the book in your hands right now has gone straight to 4 South Sudan. At the time of this writing, my goal is to raise five hundred thousand dollars for clean water, health care, education, and nutrition. South Sudan became an independent country on July 9, 2011, after the long civil war with the north finally ended. 4 South Sudan will help this new country become truly independent and prosperous.

But I have another dream for South Sudan. Shortly after the 2008 Olympics, a group of Muslim Darfurians from the University of Juba approached me about partnering with them to build a church in Kimotong. Their leader, Rudwan Dawod, was moved by my partnership with Save Darfur. In their eyes, if a Christian could speak on an international stage for a predominantly Muslim group, they should step up and stand with Christians as well. Sudan is made up of both Christians and Muslims along with animists. All of us, regardless of our different faiths, have had enough of war. In America, I saw people from all faiths come together as one united country after the attacks of September 11. That is the idea behind building a reconciliation church on the site of the outdoor church where I was kidnapped so long ago. My foundation has partnered with other groups in South Sudan with the goal of making this dream a reality and, in the process, striking a blow against the hatred that leads to war.

Twenty years ago I ran for my life as I tried to escape the soldiers with guns. Today, I run for my life as I chase down the incredible opportunity God has laid out in front of me. I was a lost boy, surviving on one meager meal a day, a boy who looked forward to garbage days because eating trash gave me the best meal of the week. Not anymore. I ran in the camp to survive. Now I run to help others not only survive, but thrive. However, I do not have to run alone. In 2014, Brittany and I exchanged our vows, becoming running partners for all the days of our lives! In marriage, we continue a celebration of love, duty, and charity. Brittany proudly serves around the world as an Air Force officer and I am training for the 2016 Olympic games. Both Brittany and I work passionately with World Vision on our partnership foundation, 4 South Sudan, bringing clean water, health care, education, and nutrition to communities in need in South Sudan. My story is unique because of my circumstances, but the end result does not have to be. You do not have to be a refugee camp survivor to run for your life and make a difference in the lives of others. At the back of this book you will find more information about how you can donate to 4 South Sudan as well as how you can get involved in the work there. That is why I run. Won't you join me?

Acknowledgments

T hanks to all my mentors, teachers, and friends who have shaped me to be the person I am today. I owe everything to your compassion and patience as I learned and grew.

I especially want to acknowledge my mentors Professor Jon Hales and Dr. Wally Rande who made me believe that I could achieve my dream at Northern Arizona University. Also, I want to thank my advisor Kim Knowles and the rest of the Hotel and Restaurant Management Department who worked so hard to support me through my education. I also want to thank my ESL teacher Ms. McNett who helped me learn to love school and finally start understanding English. A huge thanks to Tully High School teachers and staff who supported me in my journey from primary through high school in just three years. You made miracles happen!

Also, a special thanks to my coaches who shaped me as a runner and nourished my dream to become an Olympic athlete. Thanks to Coach Paccia for teaching me how to race, helping me find the fun in running, and always believing in my dream. Thank you to Coach Hayes for taking me in as part of your family and giving me the ingredients to become an Olympic athlete. Thank you to my current coach, Jerry Schumacher, for inviting me to be part of a great team and helping me realize even greater dreams in running. Finally, thank you to all of my teammates who have pushed me day in and day out and always been part of my family.

Thank you to Tom Caracci for learning my locker combination, always being there for me, and being my best friend. Thank you to Tom Hightower for recognizing my potential and challenging me to take a risk to follow my dream. Thank you to my mentors Diane Paddison, Greg Sherwood, and Steve Haas for helping me develop professionally and supporting my dream to change lives in South Sudan.

Thank you to my American parents and all my brothers for always believing in me, teaching me how to be part of a family, and most important, for giving me my childhood back. I can never thank you enough! Also, thank you to my youngest brothers, Peter and Alex, for driving me to work harder to improve lives in South Sudan and being shining examples of hard work and dedication. Thank you, Brittany for always standing at my side, sharing an amazing friendship, cheering me on, and driving me to be a world-class athlete, upstanding citizen, and college graduate. I am excited to see how our friendship continues to grow!

Thank you to Mark Tabb for helping me put my story so eloquently into words. Thanks to the team at Thomas Nelson for believing in the strength of my story and working tirelessly to share it with the world.

Finally, thank you to all of my fans and supporters. You drive me to push harder and run faster. You help me find the true joy in running!

4 South Sudan

WATER**HEALTHCARE**EDUCATION**NUTRITION**

You can help Olympic runner Lopez Lomong and others to change lives and bring healing to Southern Sudan.

World-class athlete Lopez Lomong is partnering up with World Vision to offer care, support, and a better future to families in South Sudan recovering from a legacy of warfare.

Through the **4 South Sudan** project, The Lopez Lomong Foundation and World Vision are bringing hope to families who face the realities of poverty and the lingering impact of daily violence. By providing access to clean water, health care, education, and nutrition we are providing a brighter future for the South Sudanese.

Go to **www.LopezLomong.com** to learn more and find information about how you can be involved with this great organization!